The Dance of Golf
The mysteries of movement meditation

by

Joseph K. Morgan

Published by

Zediker Publishing, Oxford, Mississippi

in conjunction with

Crystal Golfer Publications, Santa Fe, New Mexico

ISBN 0-9626925-5-7

First printing August 1995

PRINTED IN THE UNITED STATES OF AMERICA

To my Father and Mother
Willis and Florence

And with special thanks to my wife, Lena Belle

Table of Contents

"The front nine..."

Preface

The idea for a book about the integration of mind and body through golf came to me many years ago when I was a psychologist, body-psychotherapist, and scratch golfer. There had been a natural progression of background, training, interest, and experience along my personal pathways which was finally being integrated. At first I thought I needed a golf professional to cover the more technical aspects of the game while I covered the psychological side. After discussing my ideas with several potential collaborators I began to realize that the approach I was taking was radically different from the usual understanding of golf. Rather than providing any new mechanical changes (the basic grip is still the basic grip), I view my approach as being part of an evolution of consciousness, as it applies to the teaching and playing of golf. Actually, many golfers and other athletes have an intuitive understanding and knowledge of what is written here. Gestalt therapists, Zen masters, and martial art experts will be familiar with my use of energy and awareness. I hope that all of my readers will be open to explore these concepts of mind-body integration.

I have gone through another struggle in putting together this book. This had to do with personal identity. I've been a practicing clinical psychologist for over 30 years and an athlete in organized sports for 40 years. At some point these two areas in my life began to overlap. In my own mind I was becoming a sports psychologist, specifically, a golf psychologist.

The American Psychological Association has over 40 categories of psychologists, none of which clearly has anything to do with sports psychology. It seemed I was getting into "no man's land," both in the world of formal scientific psychology and in the world of sport. This became glaringly apparent to me when, after learning that a group of psychologists was having their annual meeting to discuss and share innovative techniques in psychotherapy at the famous golf resort, The Greenbriar, I submitted a proposal to do a presentation on the integration of sport (golf) and psychotherapy. My proposal was given the cold shoulder by the leadership of the conference.

I also attempted to discuss my being a golf psychologist with the Professional Golfers Association of America (P.G.A.) and was referred to several different people. Each of their reactions was essentially the same: I didn't fit into the present structure; I needed to either get my game in shape to get on the tour or to serve the necessary P.G.A. apprenticeship to become a bona fide P.G.A. golf professional. I would not have minded doing either, but I knew my contribution was different from being a tour player or a club pro. A P.G.A. representative did ask me what I had been writing. I had nothing to show at the time. I knew I had a system that worked, so it was becoming clear that one real alternative was to write the book that had been on my mind.

I am now most comfortable with the identity of "teacher." While I am both a psychologist and a professional golfer, I teach movement meditation, awareness, and higher consciousness. Golf is both the medium and the metaphor that gives purpose and direction to my teaching.

Throughout my career as a psychologist, psychotherapist, and golf teacher, I have put a major emphasis on the personal development of the individuals with whom I have worked, as well as on my own personal development. From personal experiences I have found that to live on the growing edge is always more exciting than any kind of complacency. In golf it's called "working on your game." This book is about working on your game. Not just your golf game, but the entire game of life.

Joe Morgan

February 1993

Introduction

There is great truth in the old joke "the most important six inches in golf is between your ears..." That's the part of your golf swing I want to discuss: those mysteries of the mind. However, I cannot for the life of me figure out how to discuss the brain without talking about the body, and I cannot discuss the mind without the brain. What I have done is to integrate the mind, the brain, the body, and the golf swing in a theory or system. This system of golf philosophy or psychology or "working on your game" takes into account the mind and the body. It discusses states of consciousness and their relationship to movement. Ultimately, the goal is to help people do what they intend to do.

It is important to understand that what is in this book, which is to say experiencing the ideas I am going to share, will "work." It will enable a person to play better golf, shoot a lower score. It may improve the swing, short game, and maybe even grip and stance, but people need to know up front that this is not "traditional" golf instruction. Traditional golf instruction relies on an intellectual "do this to get that" process. I'm trying to get people away from that — and about as far as possible.

There are several ways that people learn to play golf. Ideally, one learns from instructions by a professional. This is how one learns swing mechanics and finds out what "should" be happening on the course. Depending on how well the teacher can teach and the learner can learn, the student "should" become a decent golfer. We run into the problem of "what should be" not being the same as "what is." Sometimes there is a problem in going beyond mechanics or beyond the practice tee — when we actually play golf we get confused. This book may be ideal if you are like that because I want to take you beyond mechanics, beyond what is now considered traditional instruction. If you are heavily into mechanics, you may find yourself confused by this book. Confusion leads to learning and expanded awareness, so stay with it.

Much learning is done through imitation or "monkey see, monkey do." This is how children, who are open and respectful of their elders, learn and why adults need to be good role models. For adults, imitation is the cheapest and quickest way to learn; however, it short-changes the foundation our game is based on. You have to be extremely careful of who you imitate. You might just end up swinging like that person.

One of the reasons I mention imitation learning is because Ben Hogan's book *Five Lessons: the Modern Fundamentals of Golf* has left golfers of the past 40 years trying to imitate Ben Hogan. Certainly Hogan is a great role model to emulate; however, all but a few golfers have missed emulating the heart and soul of the man. They have mistakenly concentrated on "parts" of the swing, and often the more superficial parts, without grasping the whole. They have added this information to their industrial age personalities, mirroring the assembly lines of mass production. They hit one ball after another trying to create a robotic sameness that reflects the hope of the industrialized world that all things will eventually be under man's control. Do we falsely believe that our mechanics will lower our handicaps and that we can save our golf games by becoming unfeeling mechanical golf robots?

The mass-produced result is not at all like Native American artwork where every piece is different. We've gotten into sameness, but on the golf course every shot is different, every shot is unique. I'm not trying to do what I did before. I've already done that, and now I'm trying to do what I'm doing now. It's a new moment and I'm a different person. Each of us is a different person each moment, but we have a compulsive notion that things have to be repetitious, that they always have to be exactly the same. I play golf with a man who is great on the practice tee and can do whatever he wants with the ball, but when he goes on the course he's a wreck. All of a sudden his lies are different, but he's got one image, one way of doing it, and he's so caught up in trying to repeat the perfect golf swing that he's lost touch with what golf is all about. That's the problem with golf, it's not played in a bowling alley.

Superstitious learning is another one of our favorite ways to interpret the world of golf. Learning is based on results or "reinforcers." The importance of these reinforcers is based on the time schedule in which they are presented. B.F. Skinner, the famed behavioral psychologist, taught pigeons to stand on one foot by giving them a reinforcer when they stood on the foot he wanted them to stand on. The pigeon really was not conscious of what it did to get its reinforcer, but it got it so why question it? Skinner could manipulate the drive level of the pigeon by the schedule of the reinforcer. Golfers, especially self-taught golfers, are like Skinner's pigeons. We hit a good shot (reinforcer) unconsciously, and then try to attribute it to some irrelevant piece of our behavior. This is the source of some strange golf swings.

There is a hierarchy or continuum of reinforcers in golf, from the beginner's two or three solid hits from a bucket of range balls to a professional's winning the top dollar prize in a major tournament. This is one of the reasons we love golf so much. Our drive level for playing golf depends on the timing of our reinforcements. Golf is a game of intermittent reinforcement. It's like fishing: If you catch a fish each time you put your hook in the water, it becomes a monotonous chore. If you catch a fish every 15 minutes, you will find something to do for 14 minutes besides anticipating the next fish, which you know is going to strike in the next minute. It's when you don't know when you're getting reinforced — intermittent reinforcement — that really gets people hooked, and golf is like that. That's the way God works. There are a lot of similarities in how people practice both golf and religion, including a lot of superstition: *I hit the ball great when I thought this thought...* so that thought becomes something they'll try to think on every shot. Or *I had my hand over here and the ball went perfectly, so I must have to have my hand over here...* And then they wait on the next superstitious incident when they hit their next great shot. Pretty soon they have superstitious learning and superstitious minds which they prefer over confusion and real learning.

If you'll take a look at the Senior Tour players you'll see

an eclectic collection of golf swings out there. These people learned to play before the scientific analysis and cookie-cutter mentality became pervasive in golf instruction. This book is getting back to the experiential older style of learning. You are your own author or authority when it comes to you, your life, and, especially, your golf game.

The brain is such a wonderful thing to let flourish, but we don't always encourage that to happen. We are people whose minds are bound and trapped by our bodies, where the bodies become suits of emotional armor, armor that entraps as well as protects. The shape of this armor is the integrity of the person. Our armored musculature develops its own integrity, based on experience. A person takes this integrity to the golf course and that integrity determines his golf swing. He's bound by himself, and he's not going to be any better than how well he can function in that body. Play golf in control of your body, in control of yourself. It is different than being a clone, robot, or superstitious pigeon.

Please read this book through once from start to finish. Get its essence without thinking about its details. Then go back and examine the details and do the exercises. If you were to read the words contained in this book over the period of a lifetime I believe that their meanings would become deeper and more profound with each reading. The exercises in this book are most productive when first starting with the eye exercises because the energy flow goes from head to toe (more on this later).

I hope you enjoy the book and the Dance of Golf.

CHAPTER 1

The Dance of Golf

"The journey of a thousand miles begins with the first step."
Anonymous
"It might as well be a dance step."
Joe Morgan

Dance is a state of consciousness that reflects freedom, harmony, graceful movement, mind-body concentration, and rhythm. Dance is the moving expression of mind, body, and spirit. Dancing is a state of high consciousness felt by the entire body as it moves to the rhythms of the universal language of music. These rhythms permeate every cell of the body as dance is a manifestation of the embodiment of music and spirit. Dancing reflects cultural forms of social harmony, gracefulness, and oneness with God. To dance in harmony with God is to be in tune with the highest joys known to human existence.

When sport becomes dance there is an elevation of the level of consciousness and mind-body-spirit integration. Sport becomes more graceful and free-flowing. The rhythms of sport are more harmonious as sports performance becomes the performance of dance. Dance enthusiasts know the athleticism displayed by, for example, Barishnikov or the Alvin Allie Dance Troupe. The level of strength combined with the high level of balance, coordination, and harmonic movement is a wonder to observe. The reverse is also true. An avid sports fan is aware of the high level of gracefulness and rhythm involved in a long open field run by Walter Payton or a float through the air by Michael Jordan. When Johnny Miller shot a 63 at Oakmont in the U.S. Open he was literally dancing his way around the course, as was Al Geiberger shooting his famous 59. We see other athletes turn into dancers as they turn in peak performances in all sports. The Olympic gymnasts come to mind because the sport requires so many moves required from high level dancers.

Dancing is not only individual, but can also be a group effort. In my home state of New Mexico, we are blessed with many Indian cultures that practice dances passed on from generation to generation that are definitely of a spiritual matter. To observe these groups of people do a rain dance, for example, which culminates in a torrential downpour, is not unlike observing a group of athletes that band together for a sport performance that is miraculous. To watch the Suns or Bulls pull off victories in basketball by making shots that seem impossible is a lot like watching the Indians bring rain.

When the group effort brings together the physical with the mental, that has a way of making the spiritual manifest.

This is when that team is dancing!

In both individual and team sports, being a player in a dance state of consciousness is ideal and worth striving to achieve. This is a natural state of high consciousness achievable by children. How do we keep ourselves from dancing? The answer is easy: the mental, psychological, or mind aspect interferes. The main interfering culprit is known as "ego." The ego is said to be that part of our consciousness that interprets our contact with the world. The ego helps us organize our perceptual realities so that we make sense of our inner experiences and the world as we know it. It is our "own little world" we each live in. It is what makes us each unique and human. It also defends us from our ignorance, arrogance, narcissism, and other qualities that are more suitable in describing people other than ourselves. Each ego definitely belongs to the person wearing it and it may or may not be based on reality. The ego is a blessing which can also be a curse to mankind. Our minds are supposed to belong to us, yet a simple game of golf can reveal our helplessness over our minds. It is well known that golf can humble the mightiest mortal ego. Let's see how that works.

The golf game is like a Rorschach (ink blot) test. Perceptually, we project our personalities onto the ink blots, giving the blots meaning. Likewise, golfers turn their game of golf into a reflection of themselves and how they are at any given moment. In my own life I have turned the game into many types of experiences that range from nightmares to ecstasy. I have watched others on the golf course making the game spiritual or meaningless merely by their perceptions and attitudes. It became obvious that the results of my game depended on my perception, attitude, and state of consciousness.

I found that by integrating golf with movement meditation, awareness, and dance consciousness, I could be the golfer I wanted to be. By intentionally playing the game of golf in a dance state of consciousness, I have since found new rewards and pleasures on the course. I love doing the Dance of Golf. Now I would like to introduce you to the concepts behind the Dance of Golf. The steps are quite simple, yet profound. Let us first take a brief look at what is and what is *not* dancing!

The opposite of dancing consciousness is compulsive movement and intellectually-dominated behavior. Compulsive movement or intellectually-dominated movement refers to behavior which has its roots in thoughts, beliefs, and cortical (brain) patterns that are not integrated with feeling, sensation, perception, emotion, and especially, movement. When you're at a Saturday night dance at the Country Club and snuggling with your favorite partner, moving to the sounds and beat of the music, hopefully your body moves without any thought of movement. This free-flowing movement emanating from the heart is contrary to the intellectually-dominated movement so many people incorrectly use on the golf course and elsewhere. A compulsive mind is often on a power trip, or is practicing magic and superstition, or some other head game that has little to do with the task at hand.

Compulsive golf styles are directly related to compulsive

lifestyles — more is better, bigger is better. Compulsive behavior is a pervasive preoccupation with repetition, orderliness, perfectionism, and personal control at the expense of flexibility, openness, and efficiency. A compulsive person is preoccupied with details, rules, lists, order, organization, and schedules to the extent that the major point of the activity is lost.

In a compulsory education system everything is done "for your own good" whether it's really for your good or not. The teacher knows best for the student, and the student becomes obedient rather than really learning. What we get from such compulsive training are people who don't look within for their own information. Golf has also been taught that way. Our "compulsive education system" in golf has caused us to initiate the golf swing from thought patterns rather than from the heart and feet and center and core, and really experiencing yourself swinging a golf club.

Our compulsive society always seeks to change everything externally while failing to listen to their inner selves. Their compulsions drive them away from inner experience and toward an unaware, unfeeling existence. Their self-defeating lifestyles are nourished by pain, suffering, and abuse. They become embedded in a rigid ritual of meaningless repetition. Who needs it?

The Dance of Golf is a harmonious, conscious movement of a person's whole mind-body as a dancing golfer. It is done with a dancing mind and is not limited to a dance floor, golf course, or any other location. Dance can take place in the mind no matter what the activity. In the dance state one pays attention without paying attention. One moves without consciously moving. There is no split between the listener and the music, the golfer and the golf course. You experience "you" in the "what is" of the "here and now." You achieve the state of at-one-ment (atonement) or oneness of mind, body, and spirit.

In chapters that follow you will find exercises and attitudes that show you how one achieves this state of mind on the golf course. Actually, how one achieves this state in all the various activities of life can be found in this approach to golf. When you capture the essence of this book, you can find dance in your working and your loving, as well as on the golf course! A person can use the game of golf to help him become a more complete and aware human being. Not only can golf become the means of finding joy in its dance, it can also provide a way for developing and utilizing personal potential, especially in reaching peak performance. The golf shot can become a unit of personal measurement of mind-body intention, movement, integration, and awareness.

"Measurement thinking" is pervasive in our society. When we arrive at a campsite in our motorhome, all the questions from our new neighbors are in terms of numbers: what did you pay for that, how far did you drive to get here, how long did it take you, what kind of gas mileage do you get... Everything is in terms of numbers. *What'd you shoot...* We have an obsession with measurement. It irritates us and attracts us at the same time. Transcend measurement thinking, thinking beyond the numbers. How's it taste, how's it smell, how's it feel...

The little-known laws and rules of the *science of experience* can be applied to the golfer and to his unique personal experience on the course. Each golf shot becomes an experiment. More correctly, an *experiential* experiment. You are golfer *and* scientist. Your experience during the experiment is the subject matter. The science of experience requires the personal involvement of the experimenter in the experiment.

The word *experiment* is derived from the word *experience*. Albert Einstein discovered his *theory of relativity* by placing himself *inside* the experiment rather than excluding himself for "objective" reasons. By utilizing his experience as part of the whole perceptual picture, he was the first to comprehend some major relationships of time, space, energy, and movement. He did not discount or disown his own experience. In the conceptual and perceptual framework of the experiential scientist, the golfer becomes the object of study as well as the observer of the experiment. By following guidelines for objective self-observation, the "golfer-experiencer" is directed toward objective knowledge (true awareness) of self-movement, which leads to mind-body integration and conscious-intentional golf shots. This will help you reach the goal of both happier and better golf.

Observing the integration of your own mind and body on the golf course is an effective method for understanding and controlling the patterns of human movement. I have worked with mind-body integration as a healer and psycho-therapist for years, and have been witness to what many would call "miracles." For the most part, these events arise from the unification

23

of mind, body, and spirit. These miracles occur frequently in golf when we allow it. I consider hole-in-ones, some eagles, and definitely double eagles to be miracles. Normally, we do not think very much about how our mind controls our body and vice versa. This simple unawareness only reduces our production of miracles, or great golf shots. Generally, we are unaware of ourselves to the point that most of us are deluded into believing that we can move our bodies as we intend. We also believe that we have control of our minds. This is simply not true. Most of us place staggering limitations on our thoughts, attitudes, and physical abilities. We then kid ourselves with the help of rationalizations, justifications, moralizations, and externalizations. We blame the course, blame playing partners — we blame something external for our problems. *Rationalization, moralization, justification,* and *externalization* are just fancy ways of saying that we're making up a bunch of excuses to keep away from the here and now.

As some students of Zen say: the mind and the body are related like a bull rider to a wild bull, almost impossible to catch, tame, or ride. Most folks never grasp this concept, they never "see the bull." However, many good golfers I have known have begun to comprehend the nature of their rider and bull as a result of having "worked on their game." When a person struggles seriously with his golf swing, he is forced to concentrate on both body awareness and states of consciousness. This paying attention type discipline aids in the development of mind-body awareness. A person has a new level of realization or view of reality when he sees his own rider and bull.

Most golfers who can look back to shots, holes or rounds they have played in which their mental states have been extremely clear, lucid, and even spiritually inspired or guided, can recognize the ease with which they were swinging and how their mind became one with the hole, green, or the course. This is what the aware, integrated person experiences on a consistent basis. That's when you are riding your bull or at least have the bull by the horns.

A few years ago I was writing about a fictitious and mythical golfer called "Joe Hearty," a name I took from the Broadway show, *Damn Yankees*. It is also a name with which I can identify quite easily. In the story I described a 182-yard 6-iron shot in detail. Joe Hearty was in a tournament and came to the par-3 17th hole. The wind was right to left and he needed to make two or better. Incredibly, two weeks later I hit the exact shot as described in my story: a hole-in-one exactly 182 yards, 6-iron, same conditions. Normally, a person writes about a hole-in-one *after* he makes it, not before!

The fun of the hole-in-one was great. Clearly, the mystical experience for me was when I went back to my writing the following week and discovered what I had done. I had recorded my hole in one clairvoyantly. The golf shot was an example of mind-body integration. For me, the event was spiritually inspired. I had transcended ordinary time and space limitations. My essence was programmed correctly and I was dancing! Others have told me of their own mystical golf experiences. A good friend of mine played 36 holes in one day and made a hole-in-one on the same hole in both rounds. I could go on and on with similar stories. Obviously, there is more operating in the mind than most of us are able (or willing) to acknowledge. The development of personal awareness of the inner workings of your being is enlightening. Enlightenment has to do with turning on the light in your brain. The attempt to use the game of golf, the metaphor of golf, to enhance and enrich the many and diverse courses of the reader's life is enlightenment through golf.

Awareness of self as a golfer can be painstakingly slow, even boring, as one goes through the process of learning to take responsibility for his movements and to be aware of each body part and its particular movement patterns as related to the whole swing. There is a constant paying attention to the self in the *here and now*. There is the process of taking ownership of the self as it *is* in the present moment. The important point is not just to swing in a mechanically correct way, but to go a step further and be aware of the body as it moves in relation to the mind. This allows you to utilize the whole of your experience.

Two key words emerge in this regard: intention and responsibility. How many times do we *intend* to hit a shot a certain way, but somewhere between the start of the swing and contact with the ball, something interferes with our intentions and we do not do what we intended? This is a problem most of us have throughout life. We intend to do one thing and end up doing another. Sometimes we do the very opposite of what we intend. This is like the golfer hoping to make a great shot, but tops the ball instead. We would rather not top the ball, but the enemy interferes in that moment of movement and makes us do things we don't want to do. I guess we all know by now that the enemy is us.

We need to get into contact or touch with those parts of us that intervene between intention and behavior. We then need to make serious choices regarding those parts of ourselves. When the mind-body is congruent, our intentions become our behavior. When our thoughts, perceptions, emotions, neurology, and physiology are in an integrated state, functioning as one, our chances of doing what we intend to do are high. One of the most enjoyable and challenging aspects of the game of golf is that each shot is a test of our ability to do what we intend to do. It is very exciting to hit a 3-ounce ball 200 yards into a 3-inch cup with a stick. Especially when it's done on purpose!

There is also a point at which each of us needs to realize unequivocally that we are the masters of our own destiny, and that we are in fact *responsible* for ourselves and our movements of that self through time and space. That bad shot was not the fault of the guy who talked during your backswing. We are responsible for developing awareness of our perceptual world and connecting our perceptual world to the creation of intentional movement. Each golf shot is a measurement of personal intention and responsibility and saying "am I doing what I intended to do..." *Am I taking responsibility for my shot. Am I owning this sequence in my life — this unit here from start to finish. Or am I just the one who hits the good shots and someone else who lives inside of me hits the bad shots...*

This is the task of each golf shot, which becomes a reflection, projection, and expression of the whole golfer. Does the path and flight of your ball truly represent your intentions? Ask yourself — are you dancing or stumbling?

After being a serious student of how people learn and develop themselves and having also specifically observed how golf is taught at many levels, I would now like to offer a new style of teaching golf that is based on mind-body integration. It is like learning to dance which is why I call it the Dance of Golf. As a colleague once said, "You sure teach golf different from anyone else I've seen..." He had been in the golf business for 40 years. I took this as a compliment even though he was trying to tell me I was weird.

CHAPTER 2

Movement, Meditation, and Golf

"Meditation is a state of mind which looks at everything with complete attention, totally, not just parts of it. And no one can teach you how to be attentive."
J. Krishnamurti

Hitting a golf ball is best done with a clear or "beginner's mind." When each moment is as new and fresh as it is being lived for the first time. Concentration and awareness emerge and life is expressed through movement. Like golf, writing is movement expression. Writing this book is a way for me to clear my mind through movement expression. This has been unfinished business for me as it has been shaped for what seems to be such a long period of time. During that shaping there has been great

29

excitement in discussing my ideas with fellow golfers. The more I express the more I learn and grow.

In the process I have gone from an "over the hill" golfer to again playing tournament level golf. My attitude on and off the golf course has improved and I have become more positive about my life and clearer about having unlimited potential for enjoying the game. My writing seems to have been filled by so many necessary interruptions in the learning-growth process. I have invested many years of serious study in developing the book. Now the book emerges and will soon be complete. At some moment in the future, the book will fade into the background of my perceptual world. It will be finished business, soon replaced by new emergent needs unfolding in my personal drama.

Needs emerge from the whole of oneself. They organize themselves around the perceptual realities of the owner, as they pass through the process of birth-death-rebirth or organization-disorganization-reorganization. As a typical example, the need to eat emerges with great force in any hard-working golfer. The experience is a hunger, or craving sensation. The taste and feel of the full meal curbs the need. The need dies. Yet, after several more hours of hard physical work it lives again. There is an ongoing organized pattern of hunger, eating, and expression. This kind of cycle exists in the mind as well as in the body. These cycles of images, memories, and thoughts are real. In people whose mind-bodies are functioning with integration and synchronization (harmony of mind-body-Universe), these cycles run fluidly and harmoniously and are internally consistent. The person's mind is focused on the here and now, on what is, and on the awareness of self, others, and the realities of the world. There is an awareness of the constancy of change as life is expressed in verbs rather than nouns. When in this state, the eater is simply eating. There is awareness of tasting, chewing, digesting, etc. In golf, the golfer is simply golfing. Attention and concentration are pure and focused.

The space on earth occupied by any individual is his perceptual "here." Each person's present awareness takes place in a moment of experience we call "now." Awareness is paying attention. Awareness happens in the here and now — it's paying attention to what is. You're not thinking, you're being, as opposed to being divided between thoughts and feelings. When living in the "here and now" our perception of internal and external realities is enhanced. When one places the mind into the "then and there," the focus on the clarity of the present moment is muddled. To be completely in the here and now one needs to know how to pay attention to the emergent needs of the organism, and not get lost in the then and there of memory and imagination. The conscious brain-body becomes like a traffic cop who directs each emergent need along its pathway. By letting your cop be mobile, flexible, expedient, like the dancer, you can let the traffic flow without resistance! You can handle your needs as they emerge and retreat.

You can also develop a part of you which observes your thoughts and behavior as the life processes pass through you. This observer becomes your path to higher consciousness. You're developing a spiritual body that's watching you do whatever it is that you're doing. You're seeing it from the outside in rather than from the inside out.

To help you get more in touch with this process, try an exercise that has been helpful to me and to many of my students and clients. This involves repeating over and over sentences which start with words, "here and now I am _____", or, "right now I am _____". You complete the sentence by paying attention to what is at the foreground or emergent in your perceptual world. For example, "Here and now I am aware of my left little finger gripping the club; here and now I am feeling my weight shift to my right foot; here and now I am visualizing the path of my shot..." and so on. Do this for several minutes. Do this alone and with a friend as well. This is the paying attention exercise which I consider basic and fundamental to the psychology of golf. Don't allow yourself to be judgmental or critical of what emerges — just listen. It helps you get in touch with what is. The "here and now..." exercise is the stepping stone to becoming fully aware of the activity itself, which is then not an exercise but a state of mind.

"What is," is not always the same as "what should be," "what might have been," or "what could have been." Those are imaginary places in our minds. "What is," is the only thing "what" is! To discover the "what is" of your perceptual world is to get a start toward the dance of golf in its higher forms. Focus your attention on the "what is" of your grip, stance, backswing, etc. If you find yourself inadvertently getting into the "shoulds, coulds, and might haves," realize that you are putting yourself out of focus by "then and there" thinking rather than "here and now" thinking. For you to clear your mind you have to discover "what is" first. The rigid patterns and beliefs of the mind can be like a trap or jail that limits our movement, choices, and opportunities. In case you run into your own rigid, negative, abusive thoughts and beliefs, simply own them and release them with a laugh. Owning them is to accept them, acknowledge them, feel them. There is an ancient saying that a man cannot get out of jail until he knows he is in it. This applies very much to golf, and I'm talking about the golfer's mind, not an impossible lie behind a tree with traps on either side. Clearing your mind of the clutter cannot take place until you discover the clutter.

There are many ways to clear the mind. Most people I talk to never think of golf as a meditation. Some will give recognition to the peaceful states they have experienced on the course, usually early in the morning or in the beautiful moments of dusk. They view meditation as either an activity to be done during the rituals of their religion or as some esoteric form of worshipping a guru. These are both correct but are limited views based on seeing only small pieces of the whole. Because of the publicity meditation has had in past years, it is almost fashionable for modern man and woman to set aside 20 minutes a day to recite mantras, be devoted to the guru, visualize various icons, do aerobics, or practice the "relaxation response." The common thread of these activities is that they are life-positive, growth-oriented, demonstrate faith in a higher power, and are essentially mind-body oriented. I would like you to begin to view your golf game as a meditation. Playing golf is an opportunity to spend four hours in meditative, mindful activity.

This really means one thing: you begin to develop the observer in yourself. You don't really behave differently — just observe what is. This includes more than your grip or set-up. For example, by paying attention to your voice as you meet your playing partners, you listen to the words as you allow yourself to speak spontaneously. Your awareness of your voice may give you clues to your emotional state.

Suspend that compulsive or "driven by factors beyond my control" part of yourself. Observe your strengths and weaknesses. Observe your judgmentalness, your criticalness, your doubt, your limitations and negativity. Too many of us live only to get approval or attention rather than paying attention. Part of this approval game we play is to *act as if* you have a positive outlook while you attempt to cover your insecurities, anger, doubt, and negativity. Remember, it is usually easier for others to see you as you are, and for you to see the flaws of others. When you can see yourself, it is easier for the real you to be seen by others.

If you were to say, "I'm not negative," when the word "negativity" showed up, let me caution you. Observe your denial. It usually takes the form of statements that begin with "I'm not..." These "nots" are the knots in the body. Most of us have "learned to live" with our bitterness and poison. We avoid and deny this part of ourselves because this has more to do with our forms of death than life. Get in touch with how you censor yourself. See how much of your energy goes into trying to please other people. This leads to phoniness, dishonesty, and superficial, non-contactful ways of relating.

When you allow the observer of yourself to expand by letting in all of the information rather than limiting this input to positive or pleasing events, the consciousness raising process of meditation begins. You do not have to be still to meditate. Movement meditation can be done on the golf course. You can meditate for 20 minutes, two hours, or four hours. The practice range becomes a prayer chapel and the course becomes your spiritual path.

The traditions of movement in meditation are ancient and deep, passed on by various groups of worshippers. East Indian Sufis dance, sing, and chant themselves into higher states of consciousness and union with God. I knew a Hatha Yoga teacher (a yogi) who went through the postures and movements while in ecstasy and bliss. His movements reflected a clear mind open to the delights of higher consciousness that most people let pass them by. His normal day included at least four hours of yoga postures and movement, and often he went much longer. A detour here for a moment, but the following is something that might be of interest to those of you who are worried about time management. The yoga teacher worked an eight hour a day job, had a family, ran a yoga center, traveled the country teaching yoga, did four hours of postures and a couple more hours of devotional yoga each day, and in addition was a great musician. One of the keys to his high energy level was the clarity of his mind and the lack of stress. He used his time for movement as a time to rejuvenate himself. He slept only two hours a night.

When a person is not burning up his energy fighting his cluttered mind, and isn't punishing himself around the course, he is open to being nurtured by his activities, movements, or behavior. Too many of us think that all nurture comes from outside of ourselves. Think of the difference between finishing a round of golf, feeling up and ready for more life in the evening, as opposed to being washed out, drained, exhausted, ready to be fed, bathed, and put to bed like a baby. You can actually begin to let golf nurture you. Remember when we were kids and used to play from sunup to sundown? That had less to do with young bodies and more to do with young minds. Using golf as a meditation form not only helps your energy level, it makes you a more fun person to play with. You will also lower your score. It is so much easier to play when you are awake! Although meditation is relaxing, this does not imply going into a state of sleep. A person stuck in compulsive thought patterns is basically practicing unawareness or a state of sleep walking. Meditation will awaken.

Following the "what is" exercise and the development of the observer, I would like to offer you some more suggestions on mind clearing. As I have said previously, life is a continuous process of the emergence and resolution of needs. We all live somewhere between unfinished business and fulfillment, night and day, sleep and wakefulness, or heaven and earth. For the golfer, the healthy idea is for the shot at hand to be the emergent need at the time it is being played. From this perspective, a clear assessment of the shot is made and the execution of the shot is well paced and balanced. There is nothing worse than to let interfering needs distract the golfer's attention during the shot. The meditating golfer has cleared his time, his debts, his consciousness. He can play one shot at a time. His skill and experience are his background; his present shot is his foreground. Each shot is new and has life of its own. His mind is like a child's — a beginner's mind! In order to do this, one's priorities and commitments must be clear. By taking responsibility for yourself and communicating directly to your loved ones,

playing partners, and especially to yourself, you stay clear. If you want to play golf once a week, commit yourself to playing once a week. Don't come out twice a week, muddling through 18 holes with half your energy focused on your job and half on golf, while both golf and job are suffering. Taking responsibility for yourself means more than just being a good citizen, a good spouse, or good child. It means taking over ownership of your body and how (and where) you move it as well as

37

experiencing the consequences of your actions.

An excellent way of clearing the mind is to become aware of unexpressed resentments and appreciations or other personal contradictions. Once you are aware of any contradictory feelings, you can make more informed choices about expressing these feelings. This leads to better feedback and improves your internal guidance systems. The best communicators are those who have learned to say "yes" and "no" on the basis of what is organically correct for them. By organically correct, I mean choices and decisions made on the basis of somatic, or bodily, experience and awareness. For example, when choosing a club, listen to your gut reactions and your higher internal voice (which develops with self-observation) to know the correctness of your perceptions. The organism works more as a whole and in a clearer fashion when your resentments and appreciations are clear. Again, thoughts, emotions, and movement begin to line up congruently, harmoniously. Choices become clearer. Your movement in the course of your life becomes clearer. You do fewer of those activities that you resent while you develop your capacity for pleasure and life.

Finally, the practice of focusing, breathing, and walking will become the real meditative tool while golfing. This begins on the first tee as the player surveys the desired path toward the hole. His energy is then focused with all of his being and essence as he projects himself onto the ball and moves it toward the bottom of the cup. During both the swing and walk between shots, the meditative golfer focuses on breathing. As he swings, he practices on a calming centering breath. As he walks, he breathes from his nose to his toes, coordinating his breath with the walking movements. Paying attention to breathing increases awareness of other factors such as wind, distance, and especially the energy of your golf course.

    This exercise is best taught person to person. Essentially, while walking, count to four with each step being one count. While doing this, breath in for four counts, using your nose and stretching your face open wide. Now, exhale from the

nose for four counts or steps as you squeeze or grimace your face. Focus your breathing on the earth at the bottom of the hole. Smell the hole! It is with this concentrated effort that one is able to accomplish the shamanic feat of returning the white light (ball) to the center of the earth (hole). Remember, the awareness exercises suggested in this book all lead to meditative states and higher consciousness. This does not occur overnight but as a result of consistent disciplined practice, all of which can be done at the golf course.

CHAPTER 3

Quiet Mind: Quiet Putter

"Movement overcomes cold.
Stillness overcomes heat.
Stillness and tranquility set things in order in the universe."
Lao Tsu

The "short game" provides an ideal opportunity to experiment with and experience your awareness of self. Putting is meditation.

At one time I lived in Minnesota. I had a nice long hallway in my house where I could putt into one of those little machines that kick the ball back to you. During the winters I hit thousands of putts standing there in that hallway.

I learned a couple of things through that experience. One was the value of successive approximation — which I am convinced is the best way to develop true putting skills. "Successive approximation" is a psychological term that is a fancy way of saying to take one step at a time. Begin with a short putt and roll them in until you have made some predetermined number in a row. Then back up and keep going. *Make them, make them, make them, make them...* Keep backing up and keep making putts.

The second thing I learned standing in my hallway was the meditative experience of putting in that environment. Basically, putting consists of taking the putter back and hitting the proper spot on the ball and stroking it through to the hole in somewhat of an accelerating manner. When you stand in place and hit in one hundred or two hundred putts, your putting stroke never deviates — you've done a tiny, repetitious movement over and over and over. And as you do that movement it is similar to Zen sitting: you can watch the mind pass through the body. The river that flows through the body is the river of consciousness. If you watch your river of consciousness flow through you as you putt, you begin to watch all the anxieties and fears and the ways you set up to lose, the ways not to make the putt. And why would you not make it — why would you not make it every time? You don't have to practice walking down the street. There should be no worries about falling off the sidewalk, but if we began fearing that we were going to fall off the sidewalk, we'd probably start falling.

Through meditative putting, the mind begins to reveal to itself the fears and doubts and anxieties, and the only way to quiet those fears, doubts, and anxieties is to go beyond the conscious, intellectual thoughts that create them and into the sensory experience inside the body. Most of us, however, will not acknowledge that. We see the fears and come up with our own little defense mechanisms and pretend as though we don't have the fears. We hide them from other people and hide them from ourselves.

You are now aware of this fear, so how do you then quiet the mind? *Take it into your body.* Take the fear into your body and center it and ground it. Reverse the fear — begin to experience fear as excitement. Take that excitement and feel it in your heart and allow yourself to turn it into a little ball of sunshine that spreads throughout the body. Physiologically, fear and excitement are the same thing — only the intellect knows the "difference." But it's not real; it is only the interpretation of that experience. This is why some people are addicted to fear: rollercoasters scare and excite at the same time. The psycho-pathic personality craves excitement and will create it through fear. This is one root of criminal behavior, and one reason that such behavior tends to become more and more abhorrent: the need for fear induced excitement can become a deepening sadomasochistic cycle.

Some people get excitement from their own misery. The fear of winning is often the excitement of losing. The excite-ment of hitting a good shot from poor conditions is sometimes greater than hitting it down the middle. People often turn golf shots into challenges because they need the excitement at a non-conscious level. Challenges are fine, but masochistic challenges are self-defeating. Consciously, they don't like what they're doing, but the body doesn't know any different — it is getting the stimulation it wants from pain. Anxiety and fear, unfortunately, are more common than are more positive psycho-physiological parallels.

When I think about putting, the first thing that comes to mind is being quiet, learning what it means to be still. It is allowing your body to become soft and to expand, to become aware of its boundaries, its skin. It is becoming aware of the body from head to toe and feeling a movement of energy travelling downward and outward and expanding. There is a quietness or a deep settling feeling.

A deep sense of trust develops between the self and the movement expression, between the putter and the putt. When I work with a client I often hold his head in my hands. This is an exchange of healing energy that is governed by the quiet focused powers within my being and the level of trust, openness, and receptivity in the energy field of the client. My hands are expressing my consciousness. I want my energy to be clear and quiet. My mind-body being becomes like an empty vessel or like the calm water of a still pond. This is how I like to relate to my putter. When I'm transferring my own energy, I want my energy to be clear and quiet — it is like becoming an empty vessel and allowing the higher powers to flow through or letting the water inside become calm like a still pond. When I am putting I am transferring my energy or inner-ji.

I remember being in a tournament playoff with several thousand people gathered around. It was getting late in the day and it was very noisy with the gallery rushing and rallying. I had a 10-foot putt and all of a sudden everything got quiet. *Please make the noise again!* It is a very self-conscious experience being quiet out there with thousands of people watching you. What that taught me was that I had to get used to putting with my own mind. My own roar going on in my body became deafening to me.

You never make the same putt twice. It's impossible in time and space. Each sequence of behavior is a new moment, and each moment is its own moment. It is important to look at each shot as a different shot. There's a point to standing in one place and putting or standing in one place and hitting golf balls, but it's not to ingrain perfect mechanics. It's a pointless pursuit to learn to hit the ball perfectly because you will never have that exact condition again — not day to day, shot to shot, or moment to moment. You can hit 100 golf balls with a 5-iron and try to hit each one exactly the same, or you can see each shot as a unique shot. It is using two identical means to achieve radically different results. You can pay attention in the here and now and not become mechanical and repetitious. This is the experience of the indoor putting I described earlier: it is not taking the attitude of "...56, 57, 58, 59...", it is hitting putt after putt after putt

with full awareness of each moment. That's the meditation.

Wanting to hit this one just like the last one is compulsive; it is repeating rather than experiencing. Some people who have bad shots "happen to them" tend to get into a cycle of meaningless repetition, and it is the very compulsion of not making a mistake that gets them into doing it. There is a fear that one has to do something to control what happens, and that is the ultimate undoing of the person who practices in an attempt to perfect. Instead of experiencing, he compares and controls, and in doing so he loses the moment and his awareness of its worth. Do we want a world that tries to set itself up so everyone will have the same experience?

Having a good short game is really just a matter of knowing which club to use and how the ball is going to go when hit in a certain manner. Learning these things comes only through paying attention. It requires consciousness: being conscious of the shot at hand. You must be aware of the ball, the conditions, and the distance and sense what is necessary to get the ball into the hole. You can't think about what to do, you have to know what to do — you have to feel it. This comes through meditative practice.

Yips, dips, shanks, and slips are all connected to the same basic problem of being divided in some way against yourself — being confused. Massive confusion often accompanies being faced with short shots. There are so many options, so many ways to get the ball toward the hole, and the confusion comes from having so many choices. Without conviction, options cause confusion. The confusion I am speaking of is literal: it's in the brain. It is not an intellectual concept. You must reduce the options and neutralize the uncertainty. Look at the ball and see the shot you need: *where do I want it to land, how do I want it to go...* Then resolve it: play with your heart. The heart is essentially the center of the brain, and it can be smarter than the brain. When you walk up to a putt and *know* you are going to make it, that is not an intellectual process — it is the heart speaking. If you learn to listen, you will know what to do at a much deeper level. Forcing a conflict between the intellect and the heart causes division in the heart, and the confusion.

CHAPTER 4

The
Dance
Movements

"It don't mean a thing if you ain't got that swing!"
The Duke

Begin movement from your center ... move without moving.

Now I would like to introduce a mind-body or image-movement exercise leading to dance consciousness in golf. This movement is designed to teach any golfer the proper balance, rhythm, movement, and coordination required in every golf shot. It corrects weight shift, hand-eye coordination, leg movement, and the relationship of upper body to lower body in existing golf swings. It also teaches inner-outer balance and the proper use of energy, inner *ji*, or *chi*. The exercise is quite simple when done correctly, and, as is often true with many simple tasks, it may seem quite complicated at first. I will first describe the whole exercise, then describe learning it one piece at a time.

Imagine yourself as an athlete or dancer who is grounded and centered, like a Tai-chi master, NFL running back, or boxer. You are poised to move quickly and in balance. You catch the beat and rhythm of your impending movement by feeling your heart and breath. You become a medium for the energy flow from Heaven to Earth, from head to toe: a quantum of energy in cyclic vibration.

Slowly, your heart begins rocking gently from side to side, like rocking a baby to sleep. Closing your eyes, you feel the alignment of your vertebrae with the sun and the center of the earth. The vertebrae begins wagging an extended imaginary tail like a human-size prehistoric animal. The body of the vertebrae is attached to the earth in perfect balance by the platform of the pelvis-leg connection. The legs are flexed, grounded to Earth's center and fully supporting the body. The feet register a balance that resists the push and pull of outer forces. The pelvis is both free and supportive as it takes the lead in asserting movement. The hands face each other as if gripping the handle on a golf club. The arms are firm yet supple and ready to thrust like a boxer delivering a body punch with one hand or a karate chop with the other.

The movement begins slowly

with a gentle, rhythmic rocking side to side. The rocking movement gradually incorporates a turning of the shoulders as the arms move freely with the body's smooth rotation. Increasing the breadth of the motion, the feet begin to dance. The dance of the feet is done by shifting one's full body weight from left to right, then right to left, and back again, lifting each foot off the ground, slightly higher with each transition, eventually moving the knees from side to side in a kicking movement pattern. The elbows and knees move in synchronization. This is all done while the eyes are swinging from side to side or on a plane consistent with a shoulder turn. The eyes, either opened or closed, stay loose and focused. Focus can be on the sky, trees, hands, or you can go inside to focus on the inner experience. Slowly, the momentum of the body movement builds as the shoulder rotation expands and the knees and elbows lift higher and higher. You sense the unimpeded perfection of balance in natural movement.

You are no longer performing a movement — you have become a motion.

You are dancing!

■ *Warm up slowly to prepare for the Dance of Golf. Experience the feeling of coordinating eye movement with body movement, in rhythm and balance.*

This dance movement is an extension of an old warm-up technique used by thousands of golfers on the first tee. However, this movement involves much more, so please be careful to avoid underestimating it. When taught correctly, a student will learn to play and enjoy golf at a deep level rapidly.

Slowly working up to the full body movement of the exercise is the best way to learn it. This allows the body to warm up and loosens the eyes first. Start by standing comfortably. Begin looking at a point directly behind you as you turn from one side to the other. Focus only as you come to the end of the turn thus allowing the eyes to go out of focus as you are moving. Do this until you feel an ease of movement and balance. Keep the eyes level throughout the turn. Stop and rest after a minute of this. Now you are warmed up and ready to dance.

■ *Extend the warm up rotations by allowing the arms to swing on a level plane. This will be replaced with a "golfing" plane during the exercise.*

To begin the Dance, get your legs and feet in a grounded, flexed position so you are able to tilt the body forward, as when addressing the ball. Now, leading with the eyes, turn your body, picking a spot that you would see if you looked beyond your right hand on the backswing and left hand on the followthrough (for right-handers). Let your eyes swing as indicated in the previous description, focusing high above the head (use a tree or building as focal points). Most important here is making sure you are getting your support and balance from the legs. Most people are unaware of how much they rely on their eyes to "hold themselves up" and provide reference points for balance. In other words, don't be a tripod when you are a biped. The eyes have better, more mature functions.

Next in the course of learning the exercise is adding weight shift. Continuing the above exercise, add the transfer of

■ *The Harold Henning Wave mentioned in the text is the cocking and uncocking of the right wrist in the backswing. The left hand and arm moves as if turning to shake hands.*

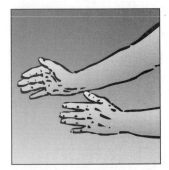

weight from left to right. When the eyes are looking right, the weight is on the right leg. When the eyes are looking to the left, the weight is on the left leg. When the weight is shifted to the right, the left hand is extended to the right as if shaking hands with a person standing next to you on your right side. The right hand does the "Harold Henning Wave" while the elbow/arm position is like a waiter holding a tray. (For those of you not familiar with Mr. Henning's post-putt trademark, refer to the illustrations.) The right hip is doing the "bump" — it is moving laterally, not just twisting back.

■ *As the weight shift is incorporated and momentum builds, the movements become more and more animated, first lifting the feet and legs, and culminating with the kicking of the feet once the knees and elbows are synchronized.*

Keep going for a minute or more! You're dancing! Maintain your balance when dancing and don't be afraid to lose it. You might lose your balance a few times before discovering where it is, but do not restrict body motion for fear of it. Dancing is a free-flowing expression of mind-body unity, not a "technique."

The whole process is reversed as the weight is shifted to the left. The left and right movements are mirrors of each other.

Gradually begin actually lifting the "weightless" leg off the ground, leading with the knee. Pull that side of the body through with the knee and elbows, keeping the knees and elbows synchronized. Reverse the process as weight is shifted. Back and forth you go until the rhythm and coordination of the

lower and upper body parts move together. When you master this much, add breathing and finally kicking.

Utilizing one's weight in the golf swing is fundamental. It is similar to other athletic moves. A place kicker or soccer kicker shifts his weight like the golfer. So do boxers, baseball players, shot putters, discus throwers, hockey players, or any other athletes involved in the throwing or kicking of a ball or object. Likewise, martial artists must be skilled in weight-shift movements.

The main cause of improper weight shift in golf has much to do with how golf is taught and how people approach hitting a ball with an object, such as a golf club. Infants learn to manipulate objects by hand and arm movement while their bodies remain helpless and incompetent. Growth occurs in a *cephalocaudal* direction (from the head downward), hence we spent a great deal of time waiting for our bodies to catch up to our heads. Our neurology is influenced by these early experiences leaving most golfers with beliefs that balls are best manipulated with hands and arms. As it turns out, the very opposite is true.

We may be intellectually convinced that golf is played with the whole body, but the neurology of movement experience is more dominant than intellectual experience for developmental reasons. When we were evolving in early experience we were all hands and head. We haven't learned to take conscious control over our bodies and are unaware of how unaware we are when it comes to intentional movement.

It is very important to feel the initial motion of dancing

grow from inside the body. Begin slowly, seeing if you can let the movement start from deep within yourself. Feel the motion in your heart and inside your brain first. Dancing comes from the inside out rather than the outside in. It starts with the heart and not with the hands!

With your eyes closed, *feel* the dance tempo of your brain. Don't visualize it — feel the movement and tempo literally inside your skull. Now let it extend and feel it in your stomach. Relax your stomach and begin to feel the tempo. Feel it all the way down into your feet.

When I say to feel the tempo inside your brain, I mean to feel it literally in the brain. There's a sense of time and space orientation. It's feedback from a guidance system that involves the ears, balance, and the pituitary and pineal glands. When a person is feeling conflict, there is a certain homeostasis that's not working right in the brain. When that conflict is resolved and integrated, it has the effect of centering the person and releasing energy that moves from the head right through to the feet. When you're not experiencing this integration, the body and brain aren't working together and you're off centered and uncoordinated. Confusion results. Confusion takes place literally at the physiological level — it's not just thoughts.

How do you know which way is up? Right now we're standing here on Earth and we're hurtling through the universe on a spinning planet. Yet, we have the illusion that we're not moving, that we're perfectly still when we really could be upside down or sideways — stillness is a delusion. We have an orientation within time and space and where we are, and when you begin to feel the tempo in your brain it's the same as tuning in to which way the sun rises and sets or which way the wind is blowing or how you find your way home.

Don't depend on your vision for orientation and balance. If you dance long enough feeling the tempo in the brain with your eyes closed, you will have a sense of swing plane and balance and all other elements in swinging a golf club that's much more sophisticated than the more mechanical or technical awareness you have through eyesight alone. I sometimes play golf with a musician who is legally blind. I've seen him hit unbelievable shots, but what's most remarkable is the way he lines up his putts. He walks to the hole and can sense through his feet which way the putt will break.

Now do this dance for 60 seconds. Do it to music playing inside your head or from a stereo at home. Coordinate your breathing — breathe in on the backswing and out on the downswing. Find the rhythm that allows you to maintain your balance. Pay attention to the movements of elbows and knees. The right elbow moves with the right knee, the left knee with the left elbow. Be aware of your swing plane and your vision. Let the eyes move on your desired swing plane. Experiment-experience different uses of eyes and balance. Find the swing plane with your eyes and your balance with your feet until you can do this dance gracefully without losing balance for at least one minute. Hold yourself up with your legs — not your eyes or head. Make the full turn with your legs and shoulders. Lead the movement with the legs and pelvis, allowing the upper body to follow. Try the Dance swinging a golf club. Let the clubhead become an extension of the arm swing and sense the same balance as if you were swinging only the arms while doing the Dance.

Now swing a club back and forth as you continue to dance. Hit some balls keeping the rhythm of "1,2,3–1,2,3" in a waltz tempo. Hit the ball on the second count of "1" while keeping the eyes focused on the ball. You should begin to feel the swing plane and tempo inside your brain.

Recreate the sensation of movement that was experienced while hitting balls the next time you begin another experience with the dance exercise.

Give yourself 10 or 20 minutes a day to practice the movements. You will begin to become aware of the necessity of balance and weight shift. You will experience more self-support from your legs. Relaxing the eyes and breath will help develop a greater awareness of life in the "here and now" lane. Let go, releasing your energy (inner ji) from heart to hand and head to toe allowing yourself to flow! Your electricity will pass through your hands to your club getting your message across to the ball. The ball responds only as it can.

Get the rhythm down pat and take it to the golf course. Dance for eighteen holes or even more. Enjoy yourself — what else would you rather be doing?

Can you walk and swing a golf club at the same time? After experience with the Dance of Golf exercises, the Dance can be "extended" into what I call the Golf Walk. In this, instead of kicking your legs as you shift your weight, you are going to take strides, moving forward, in rhythm, as you

■ *I call this series The Golf Walk. Begin by getting into the full rhythm of the Dance and then simply move forward as you continue to dance: right foot on the downswing and left foot on the back swing.*

dance. From a distance, this might appear as though you were skating on ice.

The bilateral walk, which is the coordinated "left arm, right foot" rhythm, is generated by a bilateral cerebrum. It is common in modern psychology to split the brain into left and right sides, where one controls the intuitive and the other the rational, and talk about them separately, but when both sides are working in synch we have a new product. We are using both sides of the brain in this movement.

Most people can walk in coordination without difficulty, but if I have a person lie down on a mat and make walking movements, bilateral coordination often disappears — he'll experience the arm and leg on the same side coming up and going down. This person generally has an emotional disorder or learning disability which is related to mind-gland and mind-body non-integration. Being able to experience bilateral walking when flat on the back requires connectors between the left and right sides of the brain. The common golf swing problem of a reverse pivot is akin to trying to move the same sides at the same time. Also, the "shaking hands" and "waving" hand movements in the exercises are also hard for many people to do, and it is also related to coordinating with the bilateral cerebrum. These problems can be rehabilitated with the proper exercises.

The Golf Walk is to coordinate movement, weight shift, and balance in golf that's as natural as taking a walk across the living room floor.

The Dance of Golf and the Golf Walk are *not* technical exercises designed to engineer and instill perfect swing mechanics. They are intended to offer a new awareness of motion and balance that the majority of technical exercises intended to engineer and instill perfect swing mechanics have killed off. I have people come up to me at the golf course and say, "Show me your dance..." Okay. "What's that do...help you learn to pivot..." Not exactly. The Dance of Golf is really about your attitude when the music plays: do you want to be miserable or do you want to be happy? Don't intellectualize the movements. They're not a "technique." They're a means to uncovering a different potential. Earlier when I said it was important to do the movements correctly, that did not mean that there is a clear technical objective that must be attained. Quite the contrary: the importance of doing the movements correctly is in understanding the relationship to and involvement with the whole body. You will, after experiencing the profound depth of movement, rhythm, and balance in this harmonic integration of body and spirit, discover your personal meter and the panorama that expresses your unique rendering of the Dance of Golf.

There may seem to be something missing because I don't devote a few chapters to swing mechanics, but this is a different book. Since we are talking about body movement, however, it is logical to wonder where mechanics fit. That is, after all, how you hit a golf ball, isn't it? Yes, and no.

If I'm lying on the ground and rolling my eyes around doing an exercise or squatting until I fall out on the ground, how do I relate that to mechanics, to the golf swing? What does that have to do with hitting a golf ball? What it has to do with is developing mastery over the body so that you can make the body move in the way you want it to move — golf swing mechanics included. Mechanics are nothing more than a series of muscular and skeletal movements that are necessary to strike a golf ball. There are physics involved in hitting the sort of golf shots we all want to hit, and it is unrealistic to ever think that low scores come without developing good ball striking and short game skills.

People often think that their problem is the mechanics when it's really that they don't know how to *use* the mechanics. They don't know how to feel rhythm and weight shift and use what they already know. Most of you have sufficient intellectual knowledge of the golf swing to win a U.S. Open, but what is in the head has to flow through the body for a golf swing to happen, so what you know about the golf swing doesn't really matter. The mechanics of a tense, angry golfer and those of the loose, happy golfer may be the same, but their results will likely be vastly different.

I will leave it to you to determine the form of technical mechanics you choose to support your intentions on the course. However, I will tell you that experiencing the Dance and doing the exercises will lead you toward developing good mechanics, if that is your need. Such experience will certainly prevent you from adhering to mechanics that are counterproductive to natural movement and energy flows. Be aware of your body and there will be no question if what you're doing is right or wrong.

Experience with the exercises will help a person who has an intellectual grasp of what he wants to do in the golf swing be able to actually do it. You will lose the rigidity and feeling of being bound over the ball. You will get out of your head and into your body. If you do have a mechanics problem, rest assured that the Dance of Golf will eliminate it. It will help your mechanics but it's not a mechanical issue. You can dance left-handed, right-handed, you can dance if you're ten feet tall. There are a lot of ways to hit a golf ball. Look at the senior tour: there are a lot of funny swings out there, but there are also a lot of very good attitudes — and very low scores.

It is being able to move without thinking. When I'm dancing, my body feels free and centered and grounded. Whatever is going on in the head is connected to whatever is going on in the body, and this allows maximum flexibility and extension and contact with the environment.

Right now I'm aware of... Continue doing this paying attention exercise. Be literal and concrete. Take it one thing at a time if necessary. This is a way to understand yourself, to be aware of what you are and are not!

What I want to impart is an attitude about learning that will go on and on and on. Your awareness today may be your legs and next week it may be your heart and maybe in six months you'll start seeing the ball go in the hole, all from the same exercise. It is an attitude about learning and taking yourself both as the subject and the experiment. I'm trying to impart an attitude of openness and awareness and a way of paying attention to yourself so you can make any necessary adjustments. You have choices. All the answers are in your awareness. Awareness brings consciousness. Paying attention and meditating brings an inner energy. The Chinese call it "chi," and it's a literal thing that is accumulated throughout our lives. Through awareness a person develops consciousness of chi in the body, and chi is the energy we use to send the golf ball where we want it to go. The clubhead is moving with the energy you have created and there is a sensation of directing this energy to the clubhead and to the ball. You are sending, transferring, imparting, communicating. You are taking this energy field and connecting it to the ball, letting the ball become a representative. You are sending a projection of who you are and what you are doing at that moment. Your Staff® is your staff! It's your magic wand. The golf shot is a projection of your current state. As mentioned earlier, this is using the golf shot as a unit of measurement — a measurement of mind-body intention. *Did I do what I wanted to do, how close was I, how did I feel, what was the experience?*

If you pay attention to what you experience each time you hit a ball, you get closer and closer to doing what you want to do and farther from doing what you don't want to do. It's learning how to learn, being an experiential scientist. I am a scientist: my subject is my golf game, me playing my golf game. I'm not trying to scientifically or statistically measure my performance. I'm trying to measure my *experience* in hitting a golf ball, and it is valid only for me to measure my own. You can only have your own experience and I can only have mine, and that's why it doesn't make sense for me to try to swing like you or you to swing like me. An experiment is not something that's done *to* you. You evaluate it as you do it, and you are the one who gets the record of your experience. *The awareness was confusion and the shot went short...* Try again. It's an experiment and an experience.

I described a "deep breathing" exercise earlier in the book which is done by exaggerating breathing in and out so it becomes an almost overwhelming experience. In breathing in, stretch the face and eyes wide open, breathing as deeply as you can. In breathing out, force all the air from your body, grimacing and contracting the face, pushing the air from your diaphragm. The most important understanding you should have of this breathing exercise is the level of exaggeration necessary in the effort — refer to the photos on page 39 for an illustration.

After some experience with this exercise, begin performing it as you are walking on the golf course. Through this walking and breathing exercise we're retraining the oldest, most instinctual capability within our system. We're becoming tuned in at a different level. We are tapping into the ancient layers of

the cerebrum. The olfactory-cranial nerves — those responsible for imparting our sense of smell — are the oldest parts of the brain.

I call this process of breathing and walking Stalking the Flagstick.

When the hole is cut and the greenskeeper pulls out the plug, there's a smell of earth. The nose knows! There is absolute truth in the old adage to "follow your nose." Being able to pick up that smell and zero in using a sense other than vision or knowing that "I'm 153 yards from the pin..." is a different, deeper, more intuitive and primitive measure.

Send the representation of the white light (ball) back down into the Earth (hole). It is recycled and comes back to you — everything we have the Earth gives us.

CHAPTER 5

Mind–Body Awareness

"An intricate process of limiting ability accustoms man to make do with 5 percent of his potential without realizing that his development has been stunted."

Moshe Feldenkrais

The actual golf shot takes only seconds. Hence, there is little time to think in parts while on the course in the midst of the Dance. This means that once the pieces of the swing movement have been practiced and skillfully perfected to be repeatable, it is time to act as a whole. This happens when the mind and body are integrated and expressing the whole person through the Dance of Golf.

To help understand this, let me offer a statement for you to contemplate. This is a concept that may seem simple at first and possibly easily understood; however, it will become more profound when allowed to sink in slowly over a long period of time.

A golfer's movements are based on the relationship between the internal perceptual world of the golfer and his perception of the outer world of golf.

In other words, thoughts and dreams meet physical reality creating decision-making choices of movement. However, awareness must exist for conscious choice to exist.

A high-level integration of mind-body movement includes a clear mind and an accurate, clear perception of the here and now realities presented by the external world. The optimum movement becomes a harmonious oneness between golfer and golf course. This requires great balance. Balance is needed in the relationship of the golfer's stance to the gravitational forces of Earth and also is necessary in how internal image meets external perception. Perceptions, like food, are received and digested inwardly to be expressed by movement expression as the golfer does what he intends to do. What goes in meets what is already there, then is expressed by movement. There are real advantages to becoming aware of this process in oneself. What I propose to do now is to offer some on-the-course and off-the-course exercises that will increase your ability to integrate the mind and body, hopefully leading you to more accurate perceptions and movements based on the here and now realities presented by the golfing context.

Initially, I want to bring your attention to the eyes and the breath. This is because the eyes are moved by their response to light from the outside of the body and they are moved by cortical (brain) desire and intention from the inside. This is a highly complex movement that has the effect of organizing the movement patterns of the rest of the body.

Each eyeball is connected to the body not only through cranial nerves (direct sensory connections to the brain) but also through small muscles that serve to move the eye up, down, or sideways. These muscles can hold, and do hold, tension just as other muscles of the body. The tension keeps the eye from having a full range of free movement. This is important because the eye movements are a major determinator of total body movement. To help you understand this better, I would like to offer an exercise to help free up the eyes. One quick aside first: Too much has been made of left brain-right brain functioning. It's really impossible to hit a golf ball with either one side or the other. People suggesting that you use the right side of your brain (the intuitive) when you hit the ball are naive. They essentially want people to get out of a left side dominated mode of functioning that is analytically oriented. They are partially correct. The old saying that "analysis is paralysis" is correct. What I am saying is that the whole brain is utilized during any golf shot. These mind-body type of exercises will improve left-right integration. We are after the integration of the rational and intuitive, or "holistic golf." I have a friend who told me he played holistic golf. He used the "whole" course, both sides of the rough, all the traps, ponds, hazards, trees, and he teed it up from the tips. I have something else in mind.

Now for an exercise that helps the whole brain function freely. Get comfortable (lying on your back is good but not necessary). With the eyes open, begin rotating them very slowly in small circles widening the circumference of the circle as the eye muscles get more warmed up and loose. Look with "soft" eyes: focused and aware, neither straining nor blurry. Staying in focus, briefly stop the movement at various positions along the circle. You can imagine that you are looking at a big clock and the eyes will stop at each number on the clock face. Do this in both directions for as long as you can without getting mechanical. You're becoming mechanical when you're moving and no longer paying attention to the exercise. (Such an attention lapse often occurs when exercising along with a television program: are you exercising or are you really watching television?) Do it consciously, but not by rote. Try to "feel" the eyes, let the eyes float as if the eye was like an egg yolk floating in the egg white, feeling both suspended and mobile. Allow the tears to come. Don't strain or force the eyes until you feel pain. When doing this initially you may only be able to do it correctly for 30 seconds to one minute. Keep in mind that you are not doing gymnastics or overcoming your barriers, but merely developing feel. You may eventually work up to 10 minutes or more. There is no hurry! When finished, rest the eyes for a few moments.

The next eye exercise is similar, only this time move the eyes across a giant imaginary clock so that you go from 12 o'clock to 6 o'clock, then back to 1 o'clock to 7 o'clock, then to 2 o'clock to 8 o'clock and so on. This not only helps the eyes to become free, it also begins to help you develop your ability to concentrate. Remember, from the time you walk up to the tee, take a look at the hole, determine what club you want to hit and where you want the ball to land, then get set-up and finally strike the ball, only a few minutes have passed. Do you really have control over your body for this long? Most people believe that they have control over their mind-bodies and can or should be able to carry out their intentions. This is simply not

the case. Most of us are so locked into our old cortical patterns and stereotyped movements that we might as well be walking in our sleep. Wake-up and break-out! And start with your eyes.

There is a great discrepancy between what we imagine we can do and what we can actually intentionally do. The eye exercises begin to reveal to us just how little control we have over our movements and feelings. We can check this out by keeping our observers alive and doing the awareness exercise of "what is" while we do the eye exercise.

The living body continuously breathes. This breathing, when done fully and correctly, moves the entire spine. The spine extends and flexes with each inhalation and exhalation. The ability to flex and extend the spine during the swing strongly influences the fluidity, coordination, or jerkiness of the swing.

The awareness of breath and spinal movement is inter-

locked more than most of us will ever realize. Breath is the connecting point between emotion and movement. This will be
very apparent to those of you who have played well when
among friends, but then have found yourselves in contention
in a tournament. All of a sudden there is the increased excita-
tion with thoughts of the possibility of winning. Add to that
performing in front of a larger gallery than usual and the player's breathing comes under new pressures. The stress mechanisms of the body are enacted, the mouth gets dry, the throat
feels a new pressure, the heart pulsates rapidly, the diaphragm
squeezes, the wrists thicken, and the hands shake with the
increased flow of adrenaline. This may lead to the sensation of
choking or adds a new strength that makes the golfer unaware
or in poor control over the movement of the body.

While there is really no substitute for the experience of
being in that winning position, an increase in breath awareness
off the course can prepare the golfer for this kind of added
pressure on the course. The adrenal rush that accompanies
stress can help as opposed to hurt if you practice feeling this
and have it become intentional rather than being something
that jumped up from the rough and dove inside your body.
That's the "bull." Feel that rush and excitement and take it right
into the belly. Let it expand there into positive energy and
radiate new strength throughout the body. The stress and
adrenal rush is something that's produced by your head and it
needs to flow naturally. It is an easy thing to say "let it work for
you..." but it is only through making the "body connection"
that it really can work for you. The intellectual solution to

dealing with stress — positive thinking, rationalizations, anger, and self-righteousness — is what keeps it blocked and doing its damage.

Let us now move on to the breathing exercises and also get in touch with the movements of the spine. The vertebrae of the spine move much like the archer's bow during the ideal breath. In inhalation the ends of the spine (neck and tail) flex in a backward direction. During exhalation, the movement is a forward thrust at both ends. As an example, during sexual intercourse that is coordinated in breath and spinal movement, the person breathes out during the forward thrust and breathes in during the withdrawal movement. I hope you get the picture... This suggests that a breath-coordinated golf swing consists of a slight breath in on the backswing that is followed by a slight exhalation on the downswing. I don't want to get into detail about how the pelvis is cocked at the set-up and throughout the backswing, then released and thrust forward as the player comes through the ball. Rather, just get in touch with your own vertebrae/pelvis/breath connection. Right now I want to suggest some breathing exercises to enhance your mind-body coordination.

First, lie on your back. Without making any other movement, let yourself breathe fully, without force. Breathe only through the nose. After a couple of minutes, begin paying attention to the subtle movements that accompany the breathing movement. Observe such things as the movement of the chest, the expansion and contraction of the diaphragm, the rocking of the neck, and the rocking of the pelvis. Begin

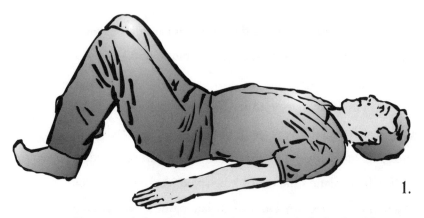

1.

■ *As you inhale, open the eyes wide, stretching the forehead and face muscles. Expand the chest and fill the stomach while rocking or curling the pelvis back, raising the small of the back and lifting the toes from the floor.*

increasing the volume of air intake by exaggerating the breath. Try to do this smoothly, without jerky movements for as long as you can. This may lead to some hyperventilation and unusual sensations. You have little to worry about unless you panic and hold your breath. Don't push yourself beyond your own level of comfort, but let yourself stretch enough to expand your awareness of the impact of your breathing. Keep in mind that each time you do an exercise, you are doing an experiential experiment in which you are the scientist and your body is the subject matter. You are both the observer and the observed. This also gives you some leeway to experiment with yourself. For example, you may want to put a pillow under the small of your back to help you get in touch with the pelvic movement or roll up a towel and place it under your neck to help you get in touch with the neck movements. Also, check out the arousal of emotion when you intensify the breathing. You may find that your mind wanders off into thinking of things that are not actually in the here and now of your experience of the movement. You may be arousing your unfinished business or this may be due to the avoidance of fear, anger, panic, or sadness. If so, bring your attention back to your body and see if you can let yourself feel the emotions rather than avoiding them.

Emotional clearing happens when the emotions are allowed to emerge and they come to completion. This may or may not occur in the early stages of doing breathing exercises. It may take weeks or months of doing this before you begin to break loose from the rigid bonds that you have placed on your body and mind.

The next exercise extends the coordination between eyes, breath, and movement. Again lying on your back, with knees up and feet on the floor and breathing fully, begin initiating a full body movement. Open the eyes wide, stretching the forehead and face muscles, expanding the chest, filling the

■ *Exhalation reverses the movement in fig 1. The stomach goes down, pushing the small of the back into the floor as the eyes squeeze shut and the face grimaces. Decrease the chest and stomach by squeezing the diaphragm, thrust the pelvis forward, putting pressure on the floor with the toes.*

2.

stomach, rocking or curling the pelvis back, lift the toes off the floor as you inhale. Reverse the movement when exhaling. As you're exhaling, the stomach is also going down, pushing the small of the back into the floor. Squeeze the eyes shut and grimace the face, decrease the chest and stomach by squeezing the diaphragm, thrust the pelvis forward putting pressure on the floor with the toes. Do this slowly at the beginning. Check out your coordination, flexibility, and smoothness of movement as you continue this deep breathing, full body movement pattern. Be aware of body awareness and unawareness. (It is important to know when you're numb, to feel that you don't feel, because this is often the first step toward attaining body awareness.) Your body may make wave-like movements as it taps the ancient layers of the nervous system.

The most primitive layers of the brain mechanisms that control movement are generally not available to human consciousness. This movement is called "involuntary" and is manifest in basically three forms. The first is the wave-like movement of orgasm, also experienced in seizure and vomiting. Other wave-like involuntary movements take place internally in our neurological, cardiovascular, and digestive systems. Our general awareness of these processes occurs only in malfunctioning times.

The second type of involuntary movement is the bilateral movement response typified by tantrums in the child and walking in adults. Neurologically, this is the opposite of orgasm. The third involuntary movement type is rest or stillness (sleeping, dreaming). A good golf swing utilizes all three movement patterns, so "involuntary" movement has a major influence on the golf game, or for that matter, all aspects of life. This is something to consider as we move on to increasing our awareness of self. How you balance the states of rage, pleasure, and calmness in your life is apparent in how you hit the ball. Hopefully, the exercises in this book lead to greater voluntary control over these "involuntary" movements.

An example of such an involuntary movement is the *cranial-sacral pump*. This is the hydraulic pumping system of the head and spinal column. Underneath the skull plates and throughout the spinal cord is the cerebral spinal fluid that the brain is encased in. This fluid runs down and through the spinal cord, all the way through to the tailbone, and back up to the head in a constant cycle. This cycle is called the cranial-sacral pump. In the average person this pump runs between 8 and 12 times per minute. Standing relaxed and normal, nothing noticeable happens. But when standing with the toes turned out, for example, it is possible to be relaxed for a time and all of a sudden there will be an involuntary, jerking type movement. That is the pump kicking in, and the reason for the jerk was that turning out the toes changed the normal spine-to-pelvis relationship and blocked the pump's normal smooth action.

An understanding of how this cranial-sacral pump operates leads to the important understanding that a golf swing should have little or no tension or rigid holding anywhere in the body. For example, too much knee bend or too much sticking the pelvis back could block the pump. The pump can be reset as easily as it can be thrown off, and neither takes much. The main point is to keep that cerebral-spinal fluid flowing smoothly.

Essentially, these exercises are done to override the overindulgent intellect and connect the brain to the body (it's attached, but not always connected).

There is an autistic aspect to everyone. Autism is a thinking disorder in which intellectual "fantasies" are not connected to reality and are unexpressed. Autistic children are extremely intellectual and have highly evolved cerebral functions, but there is so much thinking going on in the brain that it doesn't get communicated to the body. Autistic people are essentially lost in thought, which is also where many golfers are. They can think, but transferring their thoughts to their bodies is difficult.

Philosophically, we can contemplate the purpose of human kind. One obvious position that we operate from is that we occupy the Earth's surface and we serve to assist in exchanging the energetic flow of light from higher sources such as the sun to how energy is utilized on Earth. Energetically, our movements are determined by our relationship to light and gravity. Basically, we take in through our upper selves (heads and receptors) and discharge through the lower parts of our bodies. At the risk of great oversimplification, there is the process of visual perception taking place at one end of the body and the sensation or feeling of support at the other.

I would now like to add the notions of grounding and becoming centered. These are concepts familiar to dancers and martial artists as well as those who practice mind-body therapies. Neurologically, it is important not to get too polarized in the awareness of the body, but rather to remain centered. One of the methods of reducing the kind of "top heavy" polarization that comes with emotional overcharging (fear or anger), since these emotions lead to excessive thinking and poor contact, is called "grounding."

Under emotional stress, we become ungrounded and off-centered. The natural energy flow from the brain downward to the extremities is blocked and is withdrawn back into the brain. This leads to the overstimulation of the brain and activates needless thought.

When energy is stuck in the brain it leads to short-circuited loops in the human bio-feedback process. We call this "being in our heads." At this point our best bet is to get back into our bodies. Grounding is a method to get back down.

To become grounded, I will offer some exercises to "get into your legs." The feet and legs provide us with our foundation or real "under"-standing of golf. Most tension can be easily released by relaxing the neurology and letting excessive tension be drained out of the body by passing energy down through the pelvis, through the legs, and out of the feet.

Begin by standing, shifting your weight onto one foot,

■ *The flexing and squatting exercises send pent-up energy where it is supposed to naturally go — through the body from head to feet, discharging into the Earth. This is called "grounding." Stay with it until you collapse.*

bend your leg at the knee so that you begin to feel a tension in your thigh, then your knee, then the ankle and foot. Soon you may experience some shaking in your leg. Allow the leg to shake until you feel it vibrating. Switch to the other leg and do the same thing. After both legs have reached the point of vibration or shaking, relax a few moments, "feeling" the sensations of your legs.

Next, putting the weight on the balls of both feet, squat down (both legs) allowing yourself to simply feel the tension. Begin to slowly experiment in different squatting positions. Raise yourself up to different levels and hold those positions until you vibrate and finally collapse on the ground. This will lead to an increase of leg and foot awareness as well as open up the channels of energy flow in the pelvis and legs — and should help take you out of your head and down into your body. This exercise can be followed with lying completely still and paying attention to your body. Slowly allow your feet to become the focus of your attention. Let your feet get very warm or even hot. Allow any pain or tension in your body to move downward and out the bottom of your feet. You may need to be guided in this exercise if doing it for the first time. This is especially true if you have very much pain stored in your body and out of your awareness. Everyone's body has the ability to inhibit pain and make compensatory adjustments to accommodate pain so that it remains in the background of awareness. These exercises that promote body awareness will often lead to a re-emergence of old pain. To allow that pain to be felt and to be discharged is an important method of clearing out old pain leaving the mind-body in a freer state of mobility and expression.

The way to balance the body so that energy is not polarized in either direction is called "centering." An exercise in centering is in order. The center of the body is at a point just below the navel. Find that point by standing with the legs flexed slightly at the knees and relaxed, and with the concentration or focus of attention directed to this center. Try to stack the body so that each part is in alignment with the pelvis. A straight line could be drawn from the ears to shoulders to hip sockets to knee to ankles. Breathe deeply into your center while keeping in mind that, with practice, you will begin developing a greater awareness of the center of your body.

This "stacking in alignment" exercise should be continued into the golf setup position to maintain length and extension there. Starting in the upright, extended position, drop down and forward, feeling the same relationship and connection between the ears and shoulders and the pelvis. Through this, you are learning to feel the center of your body. Feel the center when upright and then feel it in the setup. Maintaining length and extension in the setup allows for better balance. Being centered is a feeling that the balance and swing are coming from the whole body — you're not top-heavy. The reason people look over the edge of a cliff and have the feeling that they're going to fall is because they are top heavy. Most of their awareness is up in the head, and looking over the edge gives the feeling that the head could fall over — all of a sudden the head feels so heavy that it is as if it could pull them right onto the ground.

Without worrying about the swing or hitting the ball, take your golfing stance — following the stacking in alignment exercise — then relax and breathe deeply down into your navel area. Ideally, you will begin feeling a surge of energy that may feel like you are aware of your digestive process in the upper intestine. It may be experienced as excitement as your awareness increases or you may feel nothing at first. You can expand on this centered feeling while hitting a golf ball. Direct your attention to only the movement of your navel while you swing. The navel moves very little during the swing so that all you need to do is concentrate on this short path the navel takes. This helps you to become more aware of the center of your swing. Another similar swing awareness exercise is to focus your attention on the movement of the heart. Again, get in touch with the heart while still. Next, pay attention to the heart movement as you make your swing. Are the movements smooth or jerky? To put your heart into your game has many implications.

Each of these exercises will increase awareness of the mind-body connection. Integrating these awarenesses with movement patterns and with "intentionality" will bring new vitality to your game. This may be awkward at first. New information tends to initially confuse a person. Remember, change is a process of organization-disorganization-reorganization. Life is a process of continual change. The amazing thing is how people tend to resist their realization of change and view their world in a static way. This is called "nominalism," the process of making verbs into nouns. Muscle tension is this process of turning dance into death. There is no split between body and mind except the one we create by our rigid beliefs, which in turn become rigid movements, and eventually, no movement. Youthful bodies are flexible, resilient, open, and soft.

CHAPTER 6

The
Mind
in the
Body

*"To know that one has been functioning in the dream is the begin-
ning of the awakening."*
Joel Goldsmith

The ability of a golfer to visualize a shot before he takes
his setup has been discussed by many of the great players of
the game. To be able to "feel" a shot and to get an instant pre-
view prior to making the shot has been a gift of the outstanding shot-makers. It is a creative process that takes place in the
relationship between the golfer and the course he is playing. It
is a good example of the mind-body connection. I would like
to discuss this process in more detail.

Over the years I've had a difficult time as a "hard" scientist figuring out just what is "psychological" or what is con-
cretely and specifically meant by something that is said to be

"psychological." We have all heard the saying that golf is 90-percent psychological. I would like to understand the 90-percent that is called "psychological." I know I'm not the only one who has struggled with this vague, abstract, almost mystical term. I have even envied those folks who don't think twice about explaining away their behavior or someone else's behavior by making the broad statement that, "It was psychological." A statement such as, "My slice must be psychological..." seems just too abstract to me. I don't mean to say that I don't get the gist of what is being said. Rather, I have spent years trying to understand exactly the nature of what is psychological. I have come to the realization that what is psychological does not exist apart from what is physical, if it exists at all. I have never seen anything psychological in an anatomy chart, or in physiology books. Psycho-physiology has mostly to do with perception, neurology, and sensation. These are very concrete processes. What I have observed most lay people attributing to the "psychological" are their politics, religion, or their basic beliefs and values. This sort of thing has more to do with group affiliation, and pecking orders, and superstitious attempts to account for ignorance. Unfortunately, these too are concrete processes.

Perceptions are based on very physical and concrete facts. What is psychological about a golf swing is also physical. There is no split in reality between the mind and the body. One can understand the mind by understanding the body. There is an energetic interplay between the physical world of light and matter and the human perceptual world which takes place in conscious awareness and in the dream state. This too is a very real physical process. How this works leads us to a greater awareness of how we can make use of visualization and other forms of perception on the course.

As was stated earlier, the human body has a basic tubular shape which takes "things" in through one end and discharges through the other end. This process is fairly obvious when discussing the digestive tract. However, this also applies to light perception and digestion of light as it forms images.

Let me get down to some basics. Light energy is passed to us from the sun. As light is materialized and formed in its various atomic patterns as earth substances, shapes, and colors, the human being interacts with this light perceptually. This occurs in the eyes primarily although the skin is also a light sensitive part of the human organism. Light patterns are taken into the body through the light and pattern receptors of the eyes. This is done through the retina by the rods and cones together with the light sensitive dilation of the pupils. This light is taken in through the cranial nerves and sent to the cortex of the brain. The brain acts as a hologram that receives a three-dimensional picture or image of a light pattern being picked up by the eye. The light activates neuronal pathways that move from the eye to the visual cortex, which is located at the rear of the brain. The visual cortex acts as a mirror or reflector of the image and feeds it back through the brain to the motor part of the cortex which is in the central part of the brain. This activates the motor centers of the brain, essentially sending messages down the spinal cord and out to the whole

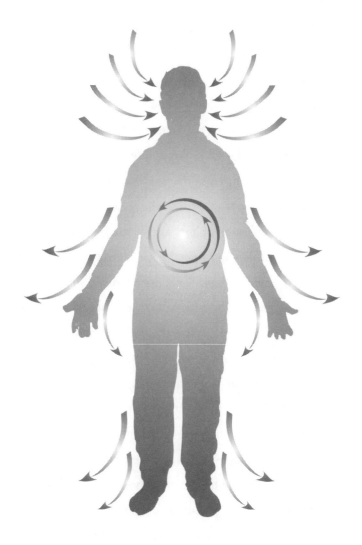

■ *Energy flows through our bodies from head to toe, circulating through the seven glandular segments and being discharged down into the earth. Light energy becomes movement. It is ones external and internal perceptions of these processes that defines the state of ones awareness — especially awareness of the internal perception. The breathing exercises prevent this natural flow of energy from blocking.*

body. The brain stem is the more primitive part of the brain.
The brain has evolved over the years by developing new lay-

ers. The neo-cortex is the "latest" layer of the brain. The latest layer has to do with our thought patterns and the structure of our reasoning. It also serves as an integrator of experience. When a golfer gets ready to make a shot, his eyes pick up the light pattern from the target. This light energy from the light source or target is sent through the eye to the brain (visual to motor cortex) and down through the brain stem to all the neural pathways connected to organs and muscles in order to activate the movement pattern as desired. These are called afferent and efferent neural pathways. One takes energy down and throughout the body and the other returns it to the brain. At a more subtle level, energy moves through meridians or the pathways utilized by acupuncture. At a more material level, energy is moved throughout the body in the blood stream and digestive system.

Our consciousness is a function of our awareness of these processes as they take place within us. Awareness can be broken down into two parts: external perception and internal perception. External perception is a recording of outside the body events as they are experienced by the perceiver within the body. Internal perception is the awareness of what takes place within the body. Within the body there are essentially two states: awareness and unawareness. Increasing awareness of the internal is essentially the new frontier of golf that is the focus of this book.

Movement is a *projection* when there is an unawareness of internal existence. Movement becomes *expression* with awareness. As a way of thinking about this, imagine that the mind-body is like a movie projector in a dark room. The projector is sending light images through a small opening, out of the room and onto a screen. This makes it appear like the action is taking place on the screen rather than within the darkroom. What has actually happened is that the action on the screen is a reflection of what took place at an earlier time when light and image were electro-chemically recorded on film. The brain is somewhat like the film. When a person is unaware of his brain or internal processes, he will live in a world of illusion, unaware of his own realities as he projects his consciousness outwardly onto whatever screen fits the needs of his internal drama. The worst part of this is that he will believe that what he sees in his outside world is "real." This is the basis of paranoia. This would be like someone going to the movies and believing that the images were real objects. They are real images, but pictures of food will not feed a starving man. Paranoid people are not nourished by their projections.

Awareness of internal mind-body processes enlightens the "dark room" of a person and changes the focus of behavior from being externally created to being internally experienced. With awareness, projection becomes expression. This makes a creative process possible that is more in keeping with universal laws of energy, movement, and growth. Intentional expression gives a person power over his own life while projection limits growth and enhances compulsive lifestyles.

Awareness leads to greater awareness as developmental processes connect to brain growth. When our brains develop, they begin to establish pathways as light is digested. The eye is the only exposed part of the brain. Sensory input, experience, and training form the pathways. These pathways are connected to memory, movement, and creativity. Who you are is a composite of these experiences. I have often compared this to the process of developing river beds in the earth. The early forming of a stream begins to move the earth's surface to shape the form of the stream or river. The neural pathways of the golfer's brain are like river beds. Some golfers are as rigid as the course of the Mississippi River. To change their golf swing would be like changing the path of the Mississippi! However, there is a great deal of power, strength, and experience in the flow of this river. The good news is that these established pathways are deep and rich and full of experience, and the bad news is that they're deep and rich and full of experience — and rigid. Young brains are fresh and easily influenced. Like young rivers, their courses of experience are fragile. How they learn golf influences movement patterns for a lifetime.

I have just simplified several textbooks of light physics, eye-brain physiology, neuro-anatomy, and sensory-motor physiology, with some overlaps into other fields such as bio-energetics. I wanted only to make a point on how the mind and body are connected. All of the sensory data being received by an organism go through similar processes.

When you get the general idea of how this process works, you begin to understand how the clutter of the neo-cortex (thinking) begins to affect movement patterns. A cluttered mind is like a hologram whose reflections from the original image are thrown off by the distortion in the mirror. There are first order, second order, third order, etc., holograms. The order is based on the degree of distortion from the original image. When you see something as it is, there is a one-to-one relationship between the visual cortex and the motor cortex. As the brain patterns are exposed to distortions (clutter) whether through trauma, training, or misperception, the perceptions of the inner or outer reality are distorted. This distorts movement, leading to movement patterns that are not those intended.

Somehow, the good Lord made us so that we adjust to our distortions and defend ourselves from feeling distorted. Most of us have been injured, abused, poisoned, scared, humiliated, discounted, and so on. We have failed to heal ourselves properly because just getting the pain under control seems good enough. This is what makes us think our movements are intentional when they aren't.

I don't know how many times I have been working with a golfer who has played just enough to begin to develop some distorted ideas on how to hold the club. I review the basic grip and place his hands in a more correct position. The first reaction is, "This feels funny." I respond, "Of course it does. You are used to your distorted hand positions." I put his hands back into place, then, three swings later the hands are way out of position again and the ball is flying every which way — but the person is more "comfortable" in the hand area. Now only the ego hurts because the ball is going wacky and the score is "too high."

To account for this we come up with "psychological"

explanations or accommodations. It seems that most folks are more comfortable not knowing themselves internally. We fail to accept that the ball doesn't lie. It responds precisely to how it is hit. As the old saying goes: garbage in/garbage out, pure in/pure out.

When you do the Dance of Golf correctly you will not only exercise and stretch the body, but you will also exercise and stretch the mind. You will bring greater purity, harmony, and balance to yourself, both internally and externally.

When I coached junior hockey I worked with kids that ranged in ages from 8 to 18. In every age group, I saw that they'd revert to their previous level of competence under stress — regression in the face of competition.

Under pressure we go back and perform the way we did at an earlier level. Everyone has had the experience of doing something new well in a relaxed environment and then finding out that pressure brought back the same old problem they thought they had fixed.

Children grow in stages, and before a child goes through the next stage of growth he will experience regression. This is evident in toilet training, for instance. We organize ourselves around our experiences. In order to grow, it's necessary to go through a period of disorganization (figuring out the new grip) and then move to a higher level (using the new grip). Although the higher level has been attained, the person is still organized around the lower level — the level he will revert to when he gets under pressure. There is no substitute for experience. None. The trick is learning to make experiences useful to you, and awareness is the key to organizing experience and making it useful.

There is a process of integrating experiences that will help get you organized at a higher level sooner. Using the grip change example, go back and remember the feeling of hitting balls using the old grip. Put that experience into your "computer." Now go to the new grip and recall the way you feel when you're hitting balls using it. Put that into the computer and then "turn it off" so you have a blank screen, so to speak. Now bring in the feelings you have with the old grip and the feelings you have with the new grip *at the same time.* Polarize and then integrate — reframe your perception of your grip. Through this integration you decide whether it should be this way or that way: new grip, old grip?

The whole crux of this chapter, and of the book itself, is to get you to be able to move without thinking. When I'm dancing, my body feels free and centered and grounded. Whatever is going on in the head is connected to whatever is going on in the body, and this allows maximum flexibility and extension and contact with my environment.

Right now I'm aware of...

Continue doing this paying attention exercise. Be literal and concrete. Take it one thing at a time. This is a way to understand yourself, to be aware of what you are and are not aware of.

What I want to impart is an attitude about learning that will go on and on and on. Your awareness today may be your legs and next week it may be your heart and maybe in six months you'll start seeing the ball go in the hole, all from the same exercise. I'm trying to give you an attitude of openness and awareness and a way of paying attention to yourself so you can make any adjustments you need to make. All the answers are in your awareness. Be that experiential person.

CHAPTER 7

The Body in the Mind

"The body speaks its mind."
Stanley Keleman

In the world of Zen Buddhism, they practice sitting. In the sitting, the meditator faces the blank wall and focuses the attention on the process of the self or mind or whatever it is that is passing through the body at the moment. The body remains quiet.

I discovered through sitting meditation that there is a connection between the garbage in my system and my feelings of interruption, distraction, and restlessness. The more of one, the more of the other. This happens in meditative golf. Ideally, the golfer's concentration is focused in the here and now, on the shot at hand. The golfer's movement seems to begin or originate from somewhere deep inside the center of his being.

The mind is clear from distraction and interruptions. The shot which has been practiced hundreds of times previously ideally goes to the target, away from trouble. Usually going down the middle of the fairway is the simplest, most direct path to the target. How we keep ourselves from going down the middle is also a function of the garbage in our systems, just like the distractions in sitting meditation. How many times have you distracted yourself from the target by giving your attention to an out of bounds, or a trap, or, especially, a water hazard? You have the impure thoughts of disaster. The golf course then practically forces you to do the very thing you're afraid of doing. The images of disaster make a bigger impression than the images of success. This kind of thought garbage is understandable. Most of us have been trained as children by fear motivation. "Watch out for that pond!" becomes, "Be careful how you hit the ball into the pond!" The assumption is that tragedy and disaster deserve more attention than the positive images of great shots. We just want to be good parents and raise good kids who do not get into trouble. We think we can keep them out of trouble by pointing out all the trouble around them. This is fine; however, it is more important to raise kids who can check out their environment for themselves. Kids who understand early in life that they need to take responsibility for their own lives, paths, movements, and, especially, consequences. We have built-in corrective systems in the human machine. These are our guidance systems, based on the mutual feedback system between ourselves and the environment. Intellectual correction by "authority" often interferes with this process leaving us with excessive internal chatter and doubts about becoming our own authorities.

The need to clear the mind of disastrous thinking becomes obvious. I am not trying to say that a person should not be aware of possible disaster, but rather, do not be consumed by it. The need to maintain the focus of one's attention on the kinds of behavior and movement that ultimately lead to success is paramount. The body which has adjusted itself to disaster tends to repeat the cycle of disaster-perception-disaster movement.

I find that most people underestimate how deeply this disaster or tragedy mentality runs within them. They try to trick themselves into having a positive mental attitude. It reminds me of wrapping garbage in a plastic sack. It covers up the smell, but the sack is still full of garbage. We all tend to be that way, some more than others. We run around with bodies full of toxic waste. We do all we can to hide this toxicity from ourselves. We put masks on our faces to cover our emotions. We gargle mouthwash to hide the stench of our digestive processes, we take antacids to quiet our stomachs, perfume our arm pits, and wear costumes that cover the realities of our bodies. I say all this not in judgement to put blame or guilt on you; rather, I want to help wake you up to the fact that you probably have more garbage in you than you realize and that it is very possible to clear it out. It is possible to get you in touch with a higher level of well-being than you ever realized previously.

Let's get to more specifics. I would like to use the analogy of alcohol intoxication. A person begins in a sober state, one in which no alcohol exists in the system. Alcohol is then consumed, let's say in a large quantity to the point where the entire organism is affected or "drunk." The alcohol is not necessary for life to go on. It does act as a brain depressant creating delusions (contractions) and illusions (expansions) of the mind which may enhance it for a bit. However, no matter how you look at it the alcohol is an essentially alien substance or more simply, garbage to the person. The alcohol then passes through the system through the process of detoxification or, in other words, the person releases it. This can be painful in a sense. The actual trauma occurs as it is ingested. The experience of pain occurs with the hangover as it is detoxified. That pain is the pain of healing as the body cleans itself. This creates the delusion which reverses the awareness of pain and pleasure. This is no different than ingesting negative images, unrealistic demands, guilt, toxic smells or food, or even toxic interpersonal relationships. It is no different than imitating incorrect movement patterns, states of emotion, or incorrect advice. Our bodies are full of tension and uptight restrictions and limitations that are based on toxic beliefs and habits. We get pain and pleasure reversed. To clear the body of garbage involves the pain of letting go of negative things that we ingest. We kid ourselves into thinking we get pleasure from our garbage, all the while crippling our bodies by keeping them full of crap, reducing our ability to do what we intend to do.

Your insides have the potential for great beauty, inner peace, harmonious movement, and divine experience. All this can take place just about anywhere you are, especially on the golf course. There is something very honest about a golf shot. If you can do it, you can do it. If you can't, you can't. You can do all the mind tricks you want with yourself or your partners but what you end up with is a score that clearly tells you what you did. There is some consistency to the statistical basis that determines your handicap. If your handicap is based on enough scores, you will have a consistent mean score and standard deviation to be expected for any particular round. In other words, you will shoot your handicap plus or minus several strokes. The garbage in your mind-body will be reflected in your handicap!

One of the best things about golf is that each of us has a handicap. The notion found in ordinary medical thinking suggests that there are some people with handicaps because of "physical" problems and then there are those who are normal. This method doesn't match up with my perception of what people are really like. From what I can tell, we each have a handicap. This has nothing to do with who is the better person. This is something like the notion of I.Q. that psychologists invented. I have seen very loving retarded people and very loving geniuses. I have seen complete jerks in the whole range of "intelligence" as well. Good and bad has nothing to do with the real notion of handicap.

The handicap in golf lets you know where you stand in relation to golf and yourself. It is a real reflection of your mind-body-spirit coordination, movement, intentionality, and responsibility in a specific task. If we assume that "working on our game" is something that is good for the whole person, we can check out our handicap and get an idea of our level of functioning. Next, we can get to work on eliminating our garbage. That is, the mental, physical, emotional, biological, chemical, and spiritual stuff inside of us that is detrimental to being quiet, focused, and harmonious during the Dance of Golf.

A better word for elimination is "release" — the letting go of the stuff of illusion, changing and moving toward the life of simplicity. After all, why complicate the golf game more than it is already? For example, not releasing the hands and club through the ball is one of the major faults of golfers who handicap themselves. This also fits with these same people, those who are not releasing their "then and there" beliefs or their bound-up emotions like fear and anger, or even their digestive wastes.

After studying myself and other human beings, I believe the first law of the Universe: what goes around, comes around, or like attracts like, or garbage in/garbage out, pure in/pure out. Energy taken into the body is either incorporated or it is passed through the human system without ever becoming a part of it. When energy is incorporated it forms an attachment to the body. When light energy is received as an image, the body assimilates the image through the electrical, chemical, and biological aspects of the brain. It is then sent downward, through the nervous system and outward to the organ and muscle systems. This is a binary system. It either makes contact with these systems or it doesn't. If it doesn't, there is no contact between the energy of the image and the appetite of an organ or muscle. The image becomes a compulsive thought, unconnected to behavior. No contact means undernourishment and unawareness. This lack of contact is due to a blocking in the neurology. This blocking is basically due to pain or trauma that shuts off awareness and reverses the movement of electrical-neurological energy. This action takes place in the electro-bio-chemical neuronal transmitter in the afferent-efferent and sympathetic/para-sympathetic nervous system. In other words, part of the nervous system is going down into the body to find out what's going on and the other is coming back to tell the brain what that is. Blocking closes this feedback loop or short-circuits the perceptual system. The usual or normal flow of energy was stopped and then mobilized to fight the trauma. Not all trauma is horrific. "Insult to organism integrity" is another way of saying "trauma." It is a traumatic thing to step up to a 3-par planning on scoring 2 and getting 6. Blowing a shot or a hole or a score can be devastating. All the expectations and praise are history.

Generally, things pass through us from head to toe. When we experience emotional trauma — anger, fear, shock — our emotions get flooded, this flow stops, and this energy that was flowing out from the brain all the way down the spinal cord and down through the feet is withdrawn. The energy in the body withdraws and comes back up into the cortex, up into the brain, so that the brain is stimulated into excessive thinking. We shut off awareness in the rest of the body. This is done to protect ourselves. It's natural to withdraw from our bodies into our brains, and that's why the feelings of numbness coincide with emotional trauma. The body of a person in shock is different from one not in shock. The give and take, the down and back, the afferent and efferent, is not happening in the nervous system. It gets stuck up in the head. The feedback loop is incomplete.

If light does make full contact, the whole body is nourished and responds by sending feedback from the organ or muscle to the brain. This may be not only nourishing, but healing where trauma exists. If the contact is made where trauma and pain have previously been blocking awareness, there is a pain that has similarities to the original trauma. This pain is the pain of healing. It is actually the reversing of a trauma-blocked area of unawareness. It is the pain of unawareness becoming awareness. This is like the hangover. For example, a person who has been forced to see images that have been shocking or fearful, which have pushed the ocular muscles (the muscles holding the eyes and used to move the eyes) beyond the threshold of excitement to the point of pain will have blocking in the eyes.

The eye muscles have reacted by becoming more rigid and unfeeling. They adapt to the anticipation of fear. They soon begin to develop a holding pattern that is based on the beliefs that would coincide with thoughts of fear. A person then compulsively seeks out external situations that will justify or make sense of the person's fearful beliefs. To be more practical: a golfer who has lost the flexibility of vision or visual feeling, possibly through an upbringing of fear, will develop rigid perceptual systems. These perceptions lead to the compulsive pursuit of rigid avoidance of fear, restricting swing movements, or it will lead to impulsive movements that seem to seek out fearful situations in a counterphobic manner. This golfer is "wild" and will have control problems. The basic problem with eyes, light, and image comes from losing flexibility in the eyes and brain. The eyes have become adjusted to trauma. This means tuning in the "then and there" of life rather than the "here and now." The "then and there" of any golf shot does not exist. You are spinning around in empty circles. Reversing the tension pattern will bring a variety of new sensations that may be uncomfortable, yet healing.

Clearing the eyes begins to clear the images and the transmission of energy through the visual center to the motor center to muscles leading to movement patterns. Likewise, clearing the olfactory sense is important to the golfer for similar reasons. The nose knows. It is important for golfers to smell the earth at the bottom of the hole. The ocular and olfactory have a similar process of receiving energy. Transmitting this energy through the perceptual system to the muscle movement system and expressing it through a clear minded, relaxed, integrated, dancing golf swing is the task. Ditto for the auditory, kinesthetic, and gustatory senses. The clearer these senses get from trauma, or "then and there" experience (or emotional blocking), the more focused, balanced, and concentrated is the effort of the golfer.

I will offer some simple, practical suggestions on clearing the body. First, seek out and give your attention to the positive, desirable, or beautiful images, both inside and out. Second, practice fasting by consuming only fruit and vegetable juices, starting with one day at the beginning. After some experience with fasting, work up to three to ten days of fasting, watching your "hangovers" as you clear out garbage. View the "hangovers" and cravings as healing. Simplify your diet. Third, begin daily stretching movements, discovering your whole body and the places where you hold on and are rigid. Work on doing the Dance of Golf each day. Next, practice sitting or lying completely still without making any voluntary movement. Pay attention and experiment with your breathing. As you do this, remain awake and check out your level of restlessness and distraction or bodily uncomfortableness. See if you can be still for 15 minutes. Work up to one hour.

Another suggestion is to try taking a look at your emotional golf game. Mentally, a four-hour round of golf is similar to running a marathon. A person starts off with a pre-game strategy or some goals that seem attainable on the first tee. There's some excitement or nervousness to go along with the anticipation of the round. Whether you feel great and are ready to tear up the course or are feeling the agony of a bad back or terminal hangover and are dreading a bad round, things start moving and changing rapidly. A few bad shots will take your mood in one direction while a series of good shots or made putts will take you in another emotional direction. Over the four hour period a normal person will pass through both highs and lows. This emotion triggers both thought patterns and movement patterns. Some of these reactions to emotions are useful and some are self-defeating. Without passing judgment on the good or bad of emotion, I would like to suggest calling on your internal observer. Allow yourself to have whatever emotions you are having. At the same time, take a position of detachment and observe and be aware of the impact of emotion on your behavior. Watch yourself be angry, elated, or bored. Pay attention to how these states affect your swing movements as well as your touch and feel.

Finally, experiment with a mind-body exercise in which you pay attention to a moment of your behavior. Do this by stating, "Right now I am _____, and that is an example of my existence!" Use first person, present tense to describe your behavior. "Right now I am completing the last paragraph of this chapter and that is an example of my existence."

CHAPTER 8

The Play of Consciousness

"Row, row, row your boat
Gently down the stream.
Merrily, merrily, merrily, merrily,
Life is but a dream."
Old Folk Song

I'd like to clarify some of the concepts I've been discussing so far — such concepts as awareness, inner light, imagery, and dance consciousness. At the time I am writing this, most people have only a vague idea of what a sports psychologist does when working with clients. Certainly, not all sports psychologists work the same way. I have had clients of all ages, handicaps, and skill and motivation levels. My favorite clients are those who are highly motivated to learn, open to self-awareness, and who realize the importance of mastering

111

and nurturing their emotions. They are also aware of their dreams and are able to report their dreams to others. If they are tournament-level golfers, that is often a bonus.

Ideally, they have sought out my services on their own. People who are pushed or manipulated into looking at their emotions create "taking responsibility for themselves" problems, often leading to early failure in their development. These individuals have a difficult time grasping the notion that they are indeed in charge of their lives. I have seen this often in youth sports. At the point of hormonal release at puberty, authority and responsibility get very chaotic and confusing. The kids are part-time children and part-time adults. The parents are part-time slave drivers and part-time nursemaids. There are ways through these problems. Take the adolescents to the golf course!

I would like to describe a typical session with someone who is already a mechanically-correct golfer and someone who meets my desired requirements as a golfer-client.

Joe Hearty is a professional golfer trying to make it through the PGA Tour Qualifying School. Technically, he knows the game and has high school, college, and mini-tour experience to prove it. He is at the point of moving up to the next level of competition, the PGA Tour. The competition is fierce so he has sought out my services to take him that extra step that is "psychological." He recognizes his pattern of getting too uptight in the last nine holes of a tournament to bring home the victory. He describes headaches and a stiffening of the neck as he comes down the homestretch. He has vague notions on what he needs to do, so we agree to get as much work done as our schedules permit.

After making the initial contract defining expectations of both mine and the client, our work involves an initial reading of body tension and body energy patterns.

Primarily, reading human energy patterns is an ability that develops with self-awareness and contacting the deeper parts of the self and others with openness and detachment. This is something that has taken me years to learn and is difficult to articulate as it takes place on an intuitive level as well as on a physical, concrete level. After assessing the client's use of energy and holding patterns, I check my perceptions out by getting feedback from the client. In this client, I see a clenching in both the jaw and the pelvis that restricts mobility and emotional freedom. With the client's permission, I demonstrate some exercises and ask the client to do these. We do eye, breathing, and relaxation exercises as we work up to seeing the inner light. This leads the client into a state of deep relaxation or para-sympathetic release. As this happens, I make him aware of visual imagery while his eyes are closed. This whole process will take 45 minutes to one hour, which is enough work for the first session. At the end of the session I usually prescribe a few exercises that are individually programmed to relieve a particular tension pattern. This is homework. He feels some instant results and looks forward to the second meeting with a better idea of what to expect from me.

By the second session I hope to have shown the client how to access to his dream level of consciousness. This is done while the person is consciously aware of both himself and what is going on around him. He is experiencing the images psycho-physiologically in the same manner as he might while in a sleeping dream state. It is a well-known fact that we all dream several times each night. This is called a rapid eye movement state or REM state and is characterized by flickering eye lids. People operate on an awareness continuum that ranges from very aware to "numb/existing." Awareness at the dream level of consciousness ranges from those who are aware of three or four dreams per night to those who are totally unaware of their dreams. For most of us, awareness of dreams fluctuates somewhere between the extremes. Most of us can recall some dreaming.

As a way of trying to be thought provoking, let me ask a couple of questions about your dreams. If your eyes are closed, in the dark of night, and you are in a state of sleep, where does the light come from that lights up the images and actions of dreams? Is the content of a dream created by the dreamer or is it just something that happens *to* the dreamer? My understanding of this convinces me that this process is internal and belongs to the person doing the dreaming. The brain stores enough electrical or light energy to produce up to 10 watts of light energy. The light energy does not leave the brain so that you can go to sleep. Internal darkness or unawareness is a creation of the neurological need to assimilate and balance both input and output. This is recharged by deep sleep.

The need for dreaming is a bit different. It is a distinct state of consciousness as is deep sleep. Watching your dreams can be like watching someone open a door to give you a peek at what is going on inside an unfamiliar house. Only in the dream state you are being given a glimpse into your own house. This is a house that serves as a foundation to all of your beliefs and attitudes. It is full of the residue of your life experiences. In the timelessness of the "dream" level you can travel both forward or backward to see where you are headed or where you have been. Spatial relationships in the dreams are not governed by gravity or by ordinary beliefs. The dream state is as under-controlled as the waking state is over-controlled. We fail to recognize or own our dreams while we take our beliefs of the external world much too seriously.

You can gain access to the "dream" state by making it conscious, taking control of it, and creating your own internal realities. When you have conscious control over this state you can see your own images or movies-in-the-head. You can see and smell flowers, hear music, or even create an internal movie of 18 holes of perfect golf. The style of your swing and round of golf will follow your deepest levels of awareness. For example, you may have a great swing yet consistently falter because you have failed to meet and recognize the monsters and demons of your inner light configurations and patterns, or your dreams. "Life is but a dream."

Joe Hearty and I meet again at a quiet, comfortable place next to the golf course where a tournament is being played. We move quickly into eye and breathing exercises and the REM state is achieved. The images begin appearing, like dreams. I now begin to guide the dream or imagery by suggestions that are related to a variety of "here and now" events that are simultaneously occurring. Without getting into detail, the images of the "dream" are significant as to color, content, direction, time, space, emotion, and so on. Knowing these things, the guide can move with the dreamer, leading at first, then, with give and take as they progress to the desired state of awareness which is the golf game of his dreams.

In the following sessions, we move more deeply into programming the unconscious or the development of new internal movies. We do outrageous visualizing that has him knocking all his putts into the hole, sinking chip shots, then short iron shots, and so on. We get into some mind-traveling and fly over the golf course where the Q-school is being held. The strategy is being planned by the whole mind-body. All we need to do now is set the body in motion on the first tee. He has already been taught how to handle the excitement of winning.

When our work together started, top ten finishes were rare. Soon there were several top ten finishes. I knew he was dancing after his third score in mid-sixties at the local PGA Q-school qualifier. He qualifies easily and moves on to the regional qualifying. Entering one's dream house or "unconscious," authoring your own dreams and taking responsibility for the whole process works in sports. Later feedback from this client indicated he was not sure how it happened, but now he is being told that he is easier to be around, more relaxed and less up-tight. He is also playing outstanding golf!

CHAPTER 9

Cosmic Golf

"There is more to being a good person than just trying to act like one."

Joeism

I would like to try to describe a state of being that I call *cosmic golf*. This goes beyond words and thoughts as the golfer plays in a state of cosmic consciousness. This is an inner organic sense of beauty, joy and pleasure that encompasses the kind of feeling found in the ecstasy of love. This is when all is right with you and the Universe, when

divine order is present in the events of ordinary life. When miracles are accomplished with ease and grace. This state is manifest in the effortlessness of a smooth coordinated golf swing

119

that sends the ball mystically toward its target. All you can do is smile as you realize that all the bumping and grinding, forcing and jerking is meaningless compared to the harmony of a swing tuned into the real forces of time, space, gravity, and coordinated human movement.

How does one describe walking up to the green, seeing with the inner eye the line, roll, and speed of a fifty-foot putt. The knowing sense that comes over the whole person as you realize deep within you that this putt is yours to have. Striking the putt knowing you are going to make it, never doubting, yet keeping this information to yourself. The inner joy is yours as you watch the ball fall into the cup. This is Cosmic Golf!

You are too intelligent and beyond belief in superstition to give credit to a new putter or to the color of your socks. You are too mature and experienced to be on an ego trip. We have all observed egocentric athletes fall off of their "high horses." You have contemplated God and the nature of a Supreme Being enough to realize that God will function on your behalf whether you make the putt or not. Actually, your experience has been one of mind-body-spirit cosmos congruence.

Remember, the laws of cosmic energy transcend all earth laws. They are more simple and more powerful. Density is a result of an increase in the number of laws governing a particular body, whether a planet or person. There is also a relationship between density and light. The more dense, the less light. At the level of cosmic law we find fewer restrictions on energy movement patterns. In the hierarchy of denseness of substance, ranging from the very dense (no light, no movement, rigid material existence) to the very light (light, movement, no materialization) cosmic law prevails over human laws. For example, the laws governing steel are more restrictive than the laws governing thought. One of our human problems is that this is perceived in reverse in where we focus our attention and values. We give little service to our cosmic consciousness while we live in our little world of material existence. When we do get in touch with cosmic consciousness and play cosmic golf we are nurturing our highest self. It is in this world that the Dance of Golf can be a source of healing. We work on our games and begin to focus on our real selves in the here and now, developing responsibility. Notice your personal energy field become bright and clear. The peace needed on Earth begins to take place within each of us. Our consciousness is motivated by a higher self rather than rewards and punishments of material reality.

Hopefully, many golfers will share this experience of mind-body-spirit cosmos congruency. Their inside world and outside world will meet and match. Each will perform small miracles. Each will have added to the goodness of the world with their positive vibrations of light, thought, and life energy. A blissful, peaceful, harmonious human being exudes that kind of healing energy. Just to be in their presence is to feel better and more positive toward life. I can't think of a better place to consciously practice this good feeling than in the beauty of a nice golf course.

My vision of the future includes an Earth-wide golf community. A community which shares higher consciousness and global awareness as it promotes communication and cooperation along with peaceful competition. Where golf courses are beautiful landscapes and gardens designed to be ecologically sound. Where people and animals will cohabitate together in peaceful surroundings. Where golf courses will become sacred places of worship and fellowship, transcending many current institutions of religious rigidity, long outmoded. It is imperative that we replace our global war games with civilized, peaceful, yet challenging games like golf. Our species needs to lower its handicap here and now.

A Few More Words

Now that you've come to the end of the *Dance of Golf*, please read it again! Hopefully, you stopped along the way and experimented with some of the exercises and, ideally, you will have made plans to devote time to this material. Believe me, it will pay off. Your experiences will lead to experiments, which will lead to more experiences. This is a process that never ends, and never should end.

This was the "front-nine." More projects are planned and one is in the works as this book goes to print. Send your name and address if you'd like notification of any new materials.

I am also available for a limited number of personal consultations — "lessons," so to speak — and encourage you to call or write if you are interested in working "one on one" or in attending one of my golf schools. I can be contacted via a communications service by writing to: P.O. Box 2190-2021, Pahrump NV 89041-2021, or by calling: 1-800-722-7468 and leaving a message for box 2021. Lena and I travel this nation continuously, so be patient for our reply.

Acknowledgements

There have been many people in my life who have shared themselves as they challenged and supported me in developing the ideas of this book.

I would like to thank them all.

I am grateful for all of the teachers in my life, especially my mentor Bob Olin, M.D. The hundreds of hours we spent doing experiential experiments have been well worth it. Also to Faust Bianco and Billy Roy, PGA Golf Professionals who were my early golf teachers at Dearborn Country Club. Thanks to my many Gestalt training therapists, especially Drs. Steve Tobin, Bob Resnick, and Abe Levitsky, who pointed me down the "here and now" path. To Virginia Satir who opened my heart and to Carol Parrish who healed my soul.

Special thanks to all of the children in my life who trusted me with their souls. My three sons, Joseph Jr., Noel, and David taught me much more than any book could have. I am very proud of each of them.

I will always remember the ten-below-zero day in Minnesota when my son Noel's squirt hockey team had an outdoor tournament. I was a parent on the sidelines when the coach asked me to help him get these 8 year-old boys to relax and get warm. We did a Sun Meditation. That was the day that this book was conceptualized. Our underdog team beat an undefeated team with grace, rhythm, and harmony! That was the day I began integrating sport and movement meditation.

Thanks also to my old golf buddies. We are family no matter how our lives change. May we remember our best shots and our best laughs.

Rather than including a formal bibliography at the end, I would like to acknowledge the influence of the following people: Fritz Perls, Georges I. Gurdjieff, Moshe Feldenkrais, Stanley Keleman, Michael Murphy, Sam Snead, Ben Hogan, Horton Smith, Coaches Ziegler, Wild, Martin, and Kitt, Bucky Fuller, Carol Parrish, Yogi Hari, Wilhelm Reich, Merle Bonney, Carlos Castaneda, John Lee Hooker, Ram Dass, Swami Muktananda, Jim Pfefferkorn, Julius Boros, Judith Aston, Bob Mathias.

I wrote the original manuscript in long-hand. I'd like to thank my sister-in-law, Lucille Martinez, for putting that through the word processor. That early copy went to a variety of people in search of continued development. Chuck Hogan took a look at it and recommended Glen Zediker. I am grateful. A big "thank you" to Glen and Kris Zediker. They have understood what I needed to bring this project to completion. I am truly grateful for this important contribution.

About the Author...

Joseph K. Morgan, B.S., M.S., North Texas State University, is a Golf and Sports Psychologist, professional golfer, writer, Gestalt Therapist, Licensed Psychotherapist, athlete, and coach. He has developed successful innovative techniques for mind-body development in sports. He has applied these techniques to develop winning individuals and teams in a variety of sports. By integrating golf with the psychology of movement, perception, and expression, he has developed the "Dance of Golf." This training program includes a variety of exercises that bring golf to the level of Yoga, Tai Chi, or in his words: "The true western martial art!"